D1346957

The Way of the Lord

Tom Wright was born in Northumberland and took a 'double first' (in Classics and Theology) at Oxford. After ordination, and a doctorate in Pauline theology, he taught New Testament Studies in Cambridge, Montreal and Oxford, in addition to working as a College Chaplain, before becoming Dean of Lichfield. His other books include *The Crown and the Fire*, *Who Was Jesus?*, *Following Jesus*, *The Lord and his Prayer* and *For All God's Worth*. He writes a regular column in the *Church Times*, and is frequently involved in TV and radio broadcasting. He is married with four children.

Also by Tom Wright and published by SPCK

The Crown and the Fire
The New Testament and the People of God
Who Was Jesus?
Following Jesus
Jesus and the Victory of God
The Lord and his Prayer
For All God's Worth

published by T & T Clark

The Climax of the Covenant

published by Lion

The Original Jesus
What St Paul Really Said

The Way of the Lord

TOM WRIGHT

TRIANGLE

First published in Great Britain in 1999 by
Triangle
SPCK
Holy Trinity Church
Marylebone Road
London NW1 4DU

© N. T. Wright 1999

All rights reserved. No part of this book may be reproduced or transmit-
ted in any form or by any means, electronic or mechanical, including
photocopying, recording, or by any information storage and retrieval
system, without permission in writing from the publisher.

British Library Cataloguing-in-Publication Data
A catalogue record for this book is available from the British Library

ISBN 0-281-05202-6

Typeset in Goudy Old Style by
Pioneer Associates, Perthshire
Printed in Great Britain by
Caledonian International Ltd, Glasgow

Illustrations by
Kerry Buck

Contents

for Richard and Jane Ninis

Preface

THIS BOOK BEGAN as a set of addresses in Lichfield Cathedral during Lent 1998. It was designed with two things in mind. First, it was to prepare a party of pilgrims for a ten-day trip to the Holy Land immediately after Easter. Writing now with hindsight on that event, it was a wonderful experience, and I am grateful to all who took part for their support and enthusiasm. I hope that giving the addresses in this new form will be of help to others in preparing for similar visits. Second, it was designed as a refresher course, from an unusual angle, on what might be called 'Christian basics'. I had in mind, among others, people preparing for confirmation, and people young or old who were feeling their way into Christian faith, and who might value a steady exposition of at least some central things that Christians believe. Again, I trust that this larger purpose will also be helped forward by making the material more widely available. In both senses, it is about 'The Way of the Lord': the way that Jesus himself took, and the way along which he invites those who follow him.

I hope and pray, in other words, that this book will help those who are going to the Holy Land to have their eyes, ears and hearts open to the many dimensions of meaning that can be found and experienced there. And I hope that it will encourage all readers, including those who are not planning such a geographical pilgrimage, to engage in the pilgrimage that really counts, joining the great company who, as St John says, 'follow the Lamb wherever he goes'. Whether you travel to the Middle East, or whether you stay at home, I hope you will find this book to contain refreshment and redirection along the ultimate pilgrim way.

A detailed note of the sources of quotations can be found at the back of the book, with due acknowledgements to those who have kindly given permission for the material to be used. Every effort has been made to trace the sources of quotations; where verification has proved impossible, I ask for pardon, and will rectify any such matters that are brought to my attention.

This book is dedicated to Richard and Jane Ninis. Richard has been my colleague for five years, as Canon Treasurer of Lichfield Cathedral and Archdeacon of Lichfield. He has given me unstinting support in my attempts to combine a ministry of writing and teaching with my cathedral work, and I am truly grateful. Jane has been the (highly successful) founder and manager of the Lichfield Cathedral Bookshop, and has probably sold more of my books than almost anyone else. Richard and Jane were members of the party that went on the Holy Land pilgrimage to which this book, in its original form, was leading. Now that they approach retirement after a long and fruitful ministry, it seems appropriate to mark the occasion with this small token of respect, affection and gratitude.

Tom Wright
Lichfield Cathedral
Feast of St John the Baptist
24 June 1998

THE HOLY LAND

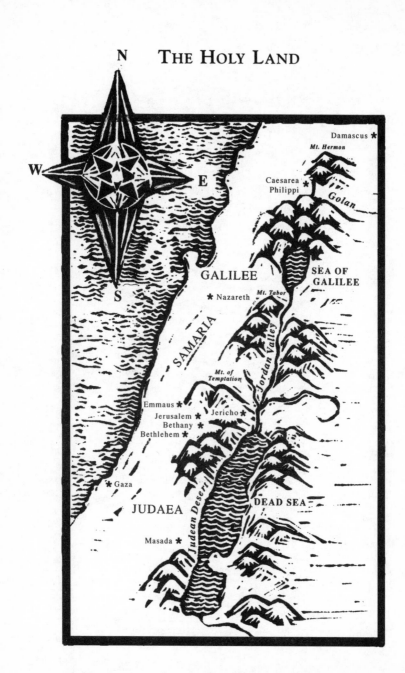

Pilgrimage Today:
A Personal Introduction

CONSIDERING MY OWN origins, it's quite surprising to me now that I didn't get into the idea of pilgrimage a lot sooner.

I was born and bred in central Northumberland, the cradle of early (and pre-Roman) English Christianity. My grandfather was Archdeacon of Lindisfarne, an island which has been a focal point of pilgrimage on and off for nearly 1500 years. Not only, however, did he not live on the island itself; never in my growing years did either the family, or the church which we attended, even consider 'making a pilgrimage' there. We went there once or twice for a day out, in the same way that we would visit Hexham, Alnwick, Bamburgh or the Roman Wall. But there was no specifically Christian or religious aspect to such a visit. One's Christian needs were considered to be well and truly met by regular worship in one's parish church, by reading the Bible and saying one's prayers. What was there to gain by going somewhere else to do the same things? The same applied to visits made from time to time to old monasteries and, indeed, to great cathedrals such as Durham. Full of history and interest, no doubt, but one was no closer to God there than in church at home, or indeed saying one's prayers kneeling beside one's bed.

I suspect there were other influences at work below the

surface. Other types of churches made pilgrimages. Ours,
being quietly but firmly of the middle-stump variety, didn't
go in for such showy things. And the people who one heard
of going on such pilgrimages were not quite our type either.
As for the Holy Land itself, sundry relatives had been to the
Middle East, during military service or on holiday. They
brought back souvenirs, but never talked, at least not to me,
about the Christian implications of such a visit. As a result,
I don't think I really thought about pilgrimage at all, or
considered it a live option. I didn't exactly reject the idea; it
just wasn't around as a possibility. Thus, though I lived in
one of the great pilgrim areas of England, I knew virtually
nothing about it.

This non-consideration of pilgrimage was strongly reinforced by the evangelical teaching I received, and eagerly
absorbed, through my teenage years. The reality and warmth
of God's presence, the wonder of his personal love for me
enacted in Jesus, the aliveness of the Bible, the enjoyment
of Christian fellowship and prayer, and the call to follow
Jesus and serve him, were quite enough to be going on with.
Within the prevailing philosophical climate, to emphasize
the 'personal' dimensions of something inclined one to
dismiss any 'institutional' dimensions as misleading or
unhelpful. Church buildings were regarded as a necessary
evil; people had to meet somewhere larger than an ordinary
house, but a large tent, or an under-used cinema, was just as
good. If I could meet Jesus Christ in a personal way in a
marquee in the Scottish highlands, why would I need to go
to a church building to continue the experience?

There was a strong sense, indeed, that 'place' and buildings
could actually get in the way. People might all too easily
suppose that going to a particular place, or going through a
particular ritual, might earn you God's favour. That was
simply another form of 'works-righteousness', drawing you

away from simple trust in what God had done in Jesus Christ. Pilgrimage spoke of mumbo-jumbo, relics, purgatory and sundry other heresies that the Reformation had thankfully done away with. In some Protestant eyes, Catholic Christians are regularly guilty of idolatry on the one hand and works-righteousness on the other. Idolatry: they worship relics, statues, buildings, reserved sacraments; they even manufacture secondary relics, according (for instance) holy status to objects, such as handkerchiefs, that have come in contact with a saint's tomb. Works-righteousness: they think that by doing certain things, going to certain places, worshipping in particularly holy sites, they will earn God's special favour, in a way that completely undercuts the biblical doctrines of grace and faith.

This way of thinking, as I met it in my teens, claimed strong biblical reinforcement, though at a cost. Had not Jesus said in John's Gospel that true worship was nothing to do with being in Jerusalem or Samaria, but was all about worshipping God in spirit and in truth? The present Jerusalem, Paul had declared, was in bondage with her children; it was the Jerusalem above, the truly free city, who was the mother of us all. This meant, of course, that all sense of continuity with the Old Testament's geographical focus, with the idea of pilgrimage to a holy city, was done away with; as with other aspects of some English evangelicalism, there was always the danger of Marcionism slipping in by the back door, however much one professed to regard the whole Bible as the Word of God. (Marcion, a second-century heretic in Rome, taught that the God of the Jews was not the same as the God revealed in Jesus, and that the Old Testament had nothing much to do with the New.)

Nobody, I think, ever challenged me on this. If they had done, I suspect I would have replied by allegorizing the Old Testament's teaching about pilgrimage, seeking a 'spiritual'

meaning in order to get around the fact that I wasn't taking
the literal one seriously. After all, any concern with earthly
institutions, let alone making a song and dance about going
on pilgrimage to them, was to be seen as part of that all-
embracing works-righteousness which the Jews had gone in
for, and which Jesus and Paul had opposed. Thus my preju-
dices, confirmed (so it seemed) on the highest authority,
remained intact. I no more contemplated going on pilgrimage
than I would have considered kissing the Pope's ring.

It is not easy to describe, let alone account for, the ways
in which my mind has changed (about pilgrimage, not about
the Pope's ring). A lot has to do with the slow turning away
from various forms of dualism, to which evangelicalism is
particularly prone, and towards a recognition of the sacramental quality of God's whole created world. Protestantism
has regularly down-played the goodness of God's created
order, on the good grounds that creation is corruptible,
subject to decay, and that if you worship it you become an
idolater. Catholicism at its best, however (and I include a
lot more than Roman Catholicism under that heading),
does not recommend the worship of creation, but the dis-
covery of God at work in creation. With the incarnation
itself being the obvious and supreme example, and the gospel
sacraments of baptism and eucharist not far behind, one can
learn to discover the presence of God not only *in* the world,
as though by a fortunate accident, but *through* the world:
particularly through those things that speak of Jesus himself, as baptism and the eucharist so clearly do, and as the
lives of holy women and men have done.

Even the cult of relics can be explained, though not (to
my mind) fully justified, in terms of the grace of God at
work in the actual physical life of a person. Even after their
death (so the argument runs) their body can be regarded as
a place where special grace and the presence of God were

truly made known. In that light, places where such saints have lived, have built churches, have been buried, become in that sense secondary relics. And, supremely, the places where Jesus himself walked and talked, where he was born, lived, died and rose again, can be seen, and have been seen by some, as effective signs of his presence and love, effective means of his grace.

Reinforcement for this line of thought has come from the surprises I have had when discovering the presence of God in particular places and buildings, in ways I had not expected. In the early 1980s, when we lived in Montreal, my elder son went to a city school which a few years before had purchased from the United Church of Canada a redundant church right opposite the main school building. Being a modern structure, it didn't look much like a church, and they used it for very un-churchlike activities, rock concerts and so forth. The first time we went there, to a very 'secular' occasion, I was stunned. I walked in and sensed the presence of God, gentle but very strong. I sat through the loud concert wondering if I was the only person who felt it, and reflecting on the fact that I had no theology by which to explain why a redundant United church should feel that way. The only answer I have to this day is that when God is known, sought and wrestled with in a place, a memory of that remains, which those who know and love God can pick up. Since then I discovered similar places which I had considered unlikely but which had the same effect.

But the supreme example, in my own life, came on my first visit to the Church of the Holy Sepulchre in Jerusalem. It was 1989. The Arab *Intifada*, the uprising against the Israeli rulers, was at its height. I flew to Israel on Palm Sunday, and spent two or three days settling in, finding my bearings, getting to know how things worked. I deliberately did not go to the Church of the Holy Sepulchre, the church built over and around the site of Calvary, until Good Friday, when I joined an early morning party walking the Stations of the Cross. I wanted my first visit to the church to be in a context of appropriate worship, not as a tourist. I had been warned, of course, of the two obvious evils which cluster in that remarkable place: competition between different denominations, and commercialization of everything in sight. They were in full evidence. Indeed, as I was standing in contemplation before the very place where Jesus was cruci-fied, I found myself elbowed out of the way by a posse of young Armenian monks, intent on their proper turn to sing an office. But I found a corner of the building with a side-chapel which seemed quiet, away from the noise and bustle; and I stayed there all morning.

And as I thought and prayed in that spot, a few yards from the place where Jesus died, I found that somehow, in a way I still find difficult to describe, all the pain of the world seemed to be gathered there. In the previous days I had seen and heard on the street the anger and pain of the Palestinians. I had seen on other streets the paranoia and painful memories of the Israelis. The very Armenians who had invaded my space carried their own memories of their own genocide, all the worse for being virtually voiceless. So much pain; so many ugly memories; so much anger and frustration and bitterness and sheer human misery. And it was all somehow concentrated on that one spot. And then, as I continued to reflect and pray, the hurts and pains of my own life came up for review, and they too all seemed to gather together with clarity and force in that one place. It was a moment – actually, two or three hours – of great intensity, in which the presence of Jesus the Messiah, at the place where the pain of the world was concentrated, became more and more the central reality. I emerged eventually into the bright sunlight, feeling as though I had been rinsed out spiritually and emotionally, and understanding – or at least glimpsing – in a new way what it could mean to suppose that one act in one place at one time could somehow draw together the hopes and fears of all the years. I had become a pilgrim.

What I discovered that day, which has stayed with me in the nine years since, is something which less rationalistic people have always appreciated, and less dualistic theologians have always embraced: that places and buildings can and do carry memory, power and hope; and that places where Jesus walked and talked, suffered, died and rose again can and do resonate with the meaning of what he did. If, of course, like the children in C. S. Lewis's Narnia stories, we go into the wardrobe to test it out as it were scientifically, we will find nothing unusual. We will come out grumbling about the commercialization, or the inadequate toilet facilities, or the price of the coffee. But if we go humbly, get down underneath the surface noise, and wait on God in the silence of our hearts, there is no telling what we may hear, what we may discover, in what ways we may be changed.

Have I, then, abandoned my earlier view that the New Testament refuses to countenance any geographical focus to Christian worship and living? No and yes. No: on the one hand, there is no such thing in the New Testament as a Holy Land. In ways that cultures other than our own seem to understand more readily, Jesus' death outside the (then) city walls seems to have brought the Land's holy status to an end. The Father now seeks worshippers from all the world, who will worship him in spirit and in truth. Yes: on the other hand, the world as a whole, and all the countries within it, are now to be regarded as holy. In the book of Acts, the whole world has become the new Holy Land, with the Church playing the role of Joshua to Jesus' Moses, going into this new land to take it captive for its rightful king.

Only, with the change from Holy Land to Holy World there goes a change in the method of its winning. If the crucified and risen Jesus is the Lord of the whole world, the weapons by which his kingdom is established are those of the gospel: suffering and love. And this kingdom will not be fully established until God acts again, finally, to implement fully the achievement of Jesus and thereby to redeem the whole cosmos. That will be the time spoken of in Romans 8, in 1 Corinthians 15 and in Revelation 21 and 22, and for that matter by Isaiah and the other prophets, the time when God will be all in all, when the whole earth shall be full of the knowledge of the Lord as the waters cover the sea. As followers of the risen Christ, we are invited both to contemplate the place where he was and to recognize that there is more to following him than geography. 'Come, see the place' is important, but must be balanced with 'He is not here; he is risen.'

We thereby arrive at what seems to me a characteristically Pauline position of now-and-not-yet. On the one hand, certain places remain special because of their association with Jesus himself, or with one of those who, indwelt by his Spirit, has lived out the life of Christ. On the other hand, the God we know in Jesus claims the entire world, and all its nations, as his own; and wherever this God is worshipped, in an igloo in the Arctic wastes or a mud hut on the equator, in a mighty cathedral or a slum hospital, in that spot another part of God's created space, as well as another moment of God's created time, is quietly claimed as his own. Our Christian living, and our Christian pilgrimages, thus take place in the space and time in between the life of Jesus and God's restoration of the whole creation. Like the sacraments themselves, pilgrimage looks back, in great acts of remembrance, and on to the time of final redemption. And with that reflection we are able once again to use the Old

Testament, with its great theme of the wandering people of God, not merely as allegory for our own spiritual journey, but as the story of the early stage in God's unfolding plan for his world.

These scattered and rambling personal reminiscences hardly amount to a full theology of contemporary pilgrimage, nor do I propose to offer such a thing here. But I want to draw these thoughts together into three propositions about pilgrimage, particularly pilgrimage to the Holy Land, which seem to me worth considering.

So that I am not misunderstood, I preface them with three warnings. First, going to holy places is neither a necessary nor a sufficient condition of being, as one might say, a good Christian. Many saints have never left their native village. Many travellers have come back worse, not better, for the experience. Think of the Crusades. Second, pilgrimage always walks on a tightrope above the abyss of commercialization. This is so whether we are in Lichfield or Jerusalem, Westminster Abbey or the West Bank. That doesn't make it invalid; it does imply that those who organize and look after holy places, and those who visit them, need to be careful about motives. Third, it remains the case that Christianity is not, at its heart, a territorial religion. It is not about conquest of lands and empires, but about God's justice and mercy reaching out to embrace the whole world in Jesus Christ and by the Holy Spirit. I believe that the just and gentle rule of Jesus Christ is vastly more beneficial in its effects on a society that seeks to live under it than any other rule in the world; but precisely this belief also prevents me from mounting military crusades against those who have chosen other ways.

So to my three propositions about pilgrimage today. I take them in ascending order of importance. First, pilgrimage to holy places has a valuable role within the Church's teaching ministry. Unless you are entirely lacking in imagination, I think you will not return from the Holy Land (and, to a lesser extent, from other historic places of pilgrimage) without fresh insight into all sorts of aspects of the biblical story, particularly the Gospels. You might, in principle, have learnt such things from books, lectures and television; but there is something about simply being there which, for most people, goes to the heart of things. People being taken round the Holy Land frequently say, 'Oh, I see – *that's* what was going on.' The sound of pennies dropping is a frequent accompaniment to Holy Land pilgrimages, and I'm not referring now to commercialization.

Second, pilgrimage to holy places is a stimulus and an invitation to prayer. Those who, like me, share the privilege of worshipping and praying regularly in an ancient holy place know well how those who come are regularly moved to pray by such a building. How much more when we visit the places where Jesus himself lived? One morning in Nazareth I walked up the hill behind the hostel and sat in the early morning sun underneath some very, very old olive trees. It suddenly dawned on me that Jesus had almost certainly climbed the same hill, and played as a boy under the same trees. I cannot describe the sense of intimacy this evoked. I felt as though I could reach out and hug him. Many feel this around the sea of Galilee in particular.

Third, pilgrimage to holy places, though neither necessary nor sufficient for Christian living, can be for many a time of real growth and depth in discipleship. This may have something to do with the sheer fact of travelling away from home, looking for something we don't yet know about. This Abraham-like existence becomes in itself an act of faith, preparing us for and sustaining us in other acts of faith. The letter to the Hebrews speaks of faith as 'the assurance of things hoped for, the evidence of things not seen', and, in the same passage, describes Abraham and the other saints of old as 'desiring a better country, that is, a heavenly one'. We are invited to join them in this pilgrimage.

This reference to a heavenly country, as I never tire of insisting, doesn't mean that the eventual future home of God's people will be in a disembodied heaven. It means, rather, that God's future reality for the world is at present kept safe in his heavenly sphere, against the day when God will bring the new Jerusalem to birth, coming down from heaven to earth, and thereby joining heaven and earth into one, rather than abolishing the latter by establishing the former. Once we've got that straight, there is every reason to regard the act of pilgrimage in itself as a metaphor, or even a sacrament, for and of the pilgrim's progress through the present life to the life that is to come. Like all sacraments, it is open to the abuse of being treated magically, as though going to a particular place automatically gains you grace, heavenly Brownie points. But the abuse does not remove the use. Our present journey really can become a means of grace, if we approach it in the right way.

My hope and prayer, then, for all who go on pilgrimage, is that they may make right use of their time of journeying: to learn new things, yes; to pray new prayers, yes; but most of all to take fresh steps along the road of discipleship that leads from the earthly city to the city that is to come, whose builder and maker is God. It is in this hope that the present book now invites its readers to follow along the Way of the Lord.

ONE

The Way to Damascus

SAUL OF TARSUS did not intend to be a pilgrim when he set off to go from Jerusalem to Damascus.

Indeed, why would any pilgrim make that journey? Pilgrims went *to* Jerusalem, not away from it. No: Saul, of course, intended to make other people into pilgrims, whether they wanted it or not. He was going to Damascus, a journey of about 150 miles as the road goes, as a matter of religious and zealous duty. He knew that in Damascus there were some Jews who had given their allegiance to a strange new teaching that was threatening, as he saw it, the very essence of Judaism. It was his task, as one who saw these things clearly, to put God's law into operation, and to seize these blasphemers and bring them in chains to the Holy City, Jerusalem itself. He would return in triumph to the presence of the living God in the Holy City, coming back along the pilgrim way with a bedraggled bunch of reluctant pilgrims in tow.

But of course Saul's journey turned into a pilgrimage none the less. A pilgrim is someone who goes on a journey in the hope of encountering God, or meeting him in a new way; and that, to his surprise, was precisely what happened to Saul. It was all upside-down and inside-out. To a devout Jew, the Temple in Jerusalem was the holiest place on earth, the place where the living God had chosen to dwell for ever. Radiating out from the holy of holies at the heart of the

Temple were, so to speak, concentric circles of holiness: the inner courts of the Temple, the outer courts, the city of Jerusalem itself, then the whole of the land of Israel. Out beyond that were the *goyim*, the pagan nations, who had so often opposed and oppressed Israel in the past, and with whom the zealous Jew would remain implacably at enmity. If you wanted to meet God, you went into the centre of those circles, not out to the edge.

In Old Testament times, one of the chief nations opposing Israel was of course Syria, immediately to the north; and the capital of Syria was Damascus, a city as ancient as most and to this day one of the political focal points of the Middle East. Between Israel and Syria there were endless border disputes, villages changing hands, skirmishes, raids and outright wars. When you stand on the Golan Heights, looking down south-west over the sea of Galilee and north-west towards Damascus, it is easy to see why trouble arose, and easy to understand the way in which the middle and late twentieth century has reproduced the same disputes, skirmishes and wars. I still remember the very odd looks my wife and I received when we drove our little rented car into a village on the slopes of Mount Hermon and stopped for a drink. The village was technically part of the state of Israel, captured in a modern war; but as far as the inhabitants were concerned it still belonged to Syria. Hostility bristles in the air in those hills, contrasting with the serenity of Galilee down to the south. When Saul of Tarsus travelled to Damascus he was, as a Roman citizen, moving from one Roman administration to another, and could do so freely; but as a zealous Jew he was going into enemy territory. He was going to do God's will, not to meet God.

But it was Saul himself, not the Damascus Christians, who became the surprised and reluctant pilgrim. As he journeyed away from the Land, away from the Holy City, away from the Temple, he was confronted by the living God: as he would later write, in a passage full of echoes of that first sight of the risen Jesus, he was faced with 'the light of the knowledge of the glory of God in the face of Jesus the Messiah' (2 Corinthians 4.6). People went on pilgrimage in order to come face to face with the living God; Saul realized the pilgrim's goal while going, literally and metaphorically, in the opposite direction.

It is as well that we should reflect on this paradox as we make our own pilgrimages. Some will be reading these lines while preparing for a visit to what we still call the Holy Land, in which case their relevance should be obvious. Other readers, though, will not; and for them in particular, though not of course excluding the first group, the deeper meaning of pilgrimage comes into focus. It has become a common-place to say that we are all on a journey: the journey of our lives, from birth to maturity and to death; and the spiritual journey of our relationship with God, which takes us, often enough, through the wilderness and the valley of the shadow of death as well as through the green pastures and beside the still waters. And as we all make that journey, starting from wherever we are and journeying, whether in obedience or disobedience, to wherever God is taking us, there are certain road-signs, certain markers on the way, for which the literal and geographical journey through the Holy Land to Jerusalem, to Calvary, and ultimately to the empty tomb, can serve as a set of metaphors or symbols.

Come back to Saul of Tarsus, blinded before the gates of Damascus. We use the word 'conversion' to describe what happened to him: and 'conversion' means, of course, 'turning round'. But it was not only Saul who was turned around in a new direction. As I have suggested, it was the very notion of pilgrimage itself. And we, as pilgrims of whatever sort, need to reflect on this conversion too.

As Saul, renamed Paul, would himself expound the point throughout his letters, Jerusalem was no longer the true Holy City. It is the heavenly Jerusalem, he wrote to the Galatians, that is the mother of us all: the coming city of God, the city that already exists in the purposes of God and will one day be revealed, with ourselves as its citizens. The earthly Jerusalem is therefore in one sense a pointer to that heavenly city, if we let it be. But in another sense, if we are not careful, it can become a potential distraction.

Likewise, the Temple in Jerusalem is no longer the true Temple. It is Jesus himself who is the place where the living God truly dwells: in him all the promises and purposes of God are summed up, not least the Temple-promise, that God will be with his people and will deal with their sin. And, equally radically, it is we who are the true Temple, because the Spirit of the living God dwells in us. The Temple in Jerusalem, therefore, along with all other buildings, however venerable or holy, is itself both a pointer to the reality and a potential distraction from it.

Pilgrimage, therefore, remains ambiguous for the Christian. Those who imagine that going on a geographical pilgrimage will automatically make them holy, or bring them closer to God, are doomed to disappointment or worse. Those who insist, today, that one part of the globe is still the Holy Land, to be claimed as a religious duty, fought over, carved up, parcelled out, and defended to the death are making exactly the same mistake as Saul of Tarsus made when, full of religious zeal, he set out on that journey to Damascus. But those who imagine that they therefore have nothing to gain from going on pilgrimage, whether to Jerusalem, Canterbury, Iona, Lindisfarne or even Lichfield, may be missing out on a pointer to the reality which we all seek. As long as we do not treat the signposts as the reality, they can remain true and helpful signposts.

The double edge of pilgrimage is summed up neatly in the two things that the angel said to the women beside the empty tomb in Matthew's account (28.6): 'Come, see the place' is balanced by 'He is not here, he is risen.' And because he is risen, ascended and glorified, we may and often will meet Jesus in the most unlikely and unexpected places: not only in cathedrals and obvious holy places, not only in liturgy and music, but in the street, the school and the slum, in the poor and the suffering, in our own Gethsemanes and Calvarys, in broken bread and poured-out wine, and indeed in our own angry journeys to Damascus.

Because the truth of the matter is that it is not we, ultimately, who are on a journey looking for God in the face of Jesus. It is God who is on a journey looking for us. How does conversion happen? You did not choose me, said Jesus, but I chose you. Our restless and wandering pilgrim hearts, as St Augustine saw, are restless precisely because the loving God has made us for himself, and we remain restless until we rest in him. And when our angry restlessness sends us off on a journey of our own making, not least when we suppose it to be part of our religious duty, we may perhaps find God coming to meet us, going in the opposite direction, so that our meeting happens like two express trains colliding. That is when you get flashes of light, blindness for three days, and a shocking about-turn, with the persecutor becoming the preacher.

There are, of course, as many ways of getting converted as there are Christians. Some of us come into the Christian faith slowly and gradually, with no blinding light or sudden revelation. The important thing, after all, is not the door by which you enter but the fact that you are now a member of the household of faith. When the Acts of the Apostles tells the story of Paul's conversion, as it does three times, in considerable detail, the purpose is precisely not to hold up

Paul's experience as a model for how everybody should get converted. Rather the opposite: Paul is seen as someone who had a dramatically unusual experience, being confronted publicly and painfully with the news that he was going in the wrong direction for the wrong reasons, and being given a commission to travel again, outside the Holy Land, into the whole world, not to bring people in chains to Jerusalem but to give people everywhere a message that would loose them from whatever chains they were already wearing, the message of freedom, of the glad love of God poured out lavishly for the whole world in Jesus the Messiah. What matters in conversion is not how, or how quickly, we are turned around from going our own way to going God's way, but that at the end of the day we have indeed been turned.

In all our pilgrimages, we begin by going back to our roots. When Christians go to the Holy Land today, we do not go because God is present there in a way in which he is not in New York or Nottingham, Lichfield or London, in Melbourne or Manchester. We go because the Holy Land is our place of roots, of beginnings; because the Lord whom we serve walked and talked in those places, laughed and wept and suffered in those places, and they carry a memory of him still, hard to describe or even to rationalize theologically, but yet of enormous power. Some have described the Land as in that sense a fifth Gospel, one which can bring the others into three-dimensional reality for us, so that we can both imagine Jesus by the lake, in the garden and on the cross, and also can sense his presence in new ways – not more or less valid than other ways, but for many a new dimension of their discipleship.

Even if we cannot do so geographically, there is still a sense in which our pilgrimage must start by going back to our roots. We need, on a regular basis, to take stock, to see where we've come from, to lay our lives before our loving God and to ask for a fresh sense of direction. We need, in that subsidiary sense, to be converted again and again on a regular basis, though of course conversion properly so-called is a unique event. We need, in prayer and reflection, to get in touch with our roots: to become aware in a fresh way of who we are and where we have come from, and particularly with how we came to Christian faith, whether gradually over many years or in a sudden blinding flash; to review what we have built upon that foundation, where we have come from in our pilgrimage.

But the important thing, when all is said and done, is to start. Few pilgrims to the Holy Land actually make the extra journey to Damascus itself. But the way to Damascus, for the pilgrim, is the way of surprising beginnings; and it may be that some readers need to make a new and surprising beginning right now, meeting God in Christ either for the first time or in a quite fresh way. Such a meeting is always humbling, and we resist it for that reason; even to mention conversion within an established church (in both senses) can feel like a serious social gaffe. But conversion does happen, and often to unlikely people at unlikely moments, including some deeply religious people whose religion had actually been, as Paul's was, a screen hiding them from the loving face of the living God. It can happen to anyone. It can happen to you.

For some, it happens as the re-awakening of a spirituality long dormant or forgotten. The writer Edwin Muir, at around the age of fifty, wrote the following one day in his diary:

Last night, going to bed alone, I suddenly found myself (I was taking off my waistcoat) reciting the Lord's Prayer in a loud, emphatic voice – a thing I had not done for many years – with deep urgency and profound disturbed emotion. While I went on I grew more composed; as if it had been empty and craving and were being replenished, my soul grew still; every word had a strange fullness of meaning which astonished and delighted me. It was late; I had sat up reading; I was sleepy; but as I stood in the middle of the floor half-undressed, saying the prayer over and over, meaning after meaning sprang from it, overcoming me again with joyful surprise . . .

For others, it happens as dramatically as it did for Saul of Tarsus, confronting them, turning them round, and sending them off in the opposite direction. Around the time Muir was rediscovering the power of the Lord's Prayer, a young Russian communist went to a meeting one night where he heard a Christian expounding his faith. The communist was angry. How could anyone still believe such nonsensical superstition in these days? He went home, determined to write a refutation of Christianity that would settle the issue once and for all. In order to get the quarry properly into his sights, he found an old Bible and looked into it. He didn't want to waste more time than was necessary, so he decided to read the shortest of the four Gospels, that of St Mark. It was only much later, as he said, that he realized that God has a sense of humour. St Mark's Gospel is exactly the book written for someone in that frame of mind: pulling no punches, getting directly to the point, portraying Jesus the Messiah bringing through his death and resurrection a kingdom that outshines all the political dreams of the world. He read Mark again, then the other Gospels; then, sitting up through the night, the rest of the New Testament. By morning he was a believing, praying Christian. That man is Anthony Bloom, who went on to become one of the great Russian Orthodox bishops of our generation, leading his flock through intense suffering but always seeing and reflecting the glory of God in the face of Jesus.

Consider, finally, that in some ways typical and sometimes muddled Anglican, John Betjeman. In 1955 a leading humanist gave a series of broadcasts attacking Christianity. Betjeman, in characteristically understated fashion, replied by reflecting on the conversion of St Paul, and on conversion in general:

> . . .
> Saint Paul is often criticised
> By modern people who're annoyed
> At his conversion, saying Freud
> Explains it all. But they omit
> The really vital point of it,
> Which isn't *how* it was achieved,
> But what it was that Paul believed.
> . . .
> What is conversion? Not at all
> For me the experience of St Paul,
> No blinding light, a fitful glow
> Is all the light of faith I know
> Which sometimes goes completely out
> And leaves me plunging round in doubt
> Until I will myself to go
> And worship in God's house below –
> My parish church – and even there
> I find distractions everywhere.
> . . .
> What is Conversion? Turning round
> To gaze upon a love profound.
> For some of us see Jesus plain
> And never once look back again,
> And some of us have seen and known

And turned and gone away alone,
But most of us turn slow to see
The figure hanging on a tree
And stumble on and blindly grope
Upheld by intermittent hope.
God grant before we die we all
May see the light as did St Paul.

My prayer, then, is that our pilgrimages, both outward and inward, may bring us face to face with the one in whom we see the love of God turned toward us, and send us on our way to serve him afresh in his world.

TWO

The Way to the Jordan

THE WAY TO the Promised Land lies through the Jordan. That was how it always was, and that is how it always will be. The route thus brings us to the banks of one of the most famous rivers in the world.

These days it's quite a scruffy little river. It's not, in any case, very long: only about twenty miles from its source on the southern slopes of Mount Hermon down to the lake variously called Gennesaret (because of its shape like a harp, in Hebrew *Kinnor*), or the Sea of Galilee; and then about another sixty miles from the Sea of Galilee south to the Dead Sea, the lowest point on the earth. And though in spring, when the snows melt on Mount Hermon, and Galilee gets plenty of rain, the river can sometimes still swell to quite a torrent, the Israeli government has piped so much water from it that it often seems not much more than a muddy stream. By the time it gets to Jericho there is so little water that the Dead Sea itself has, in recent years, begun to dry up, and has actually changed shape; the inflow can no longer keep up with evaporation. Ezekiel prophesied that the Dead Sea would become fresh, and that people would fish in it; but, if things go on the way they are, the time will come when they will build houses and roads on the dry land where it used to be.

Even in biblical times, it appears, the Jordan wasn't that impressive. In the famous story in 2 Kings 5, Naaman, the commander of the Syrian (or 'Aramean') army, compares it

25

unfavourably with Abana and Pharpar, the rivers which rise on the north-eastern slopes of Mount Hermon and make their way towards Damascus. But something more than a geographer's comparison is at stake here. It's a matter of national pride, and, underneath that, a clash of gods. Naaman was a loyal Syrian, and he worshipped the Syrian god Rimmon. Coming south to Israel, he knew of the Israelite god Yahweh; and his comparison of Rimmon's rivers and Yahweh's river was another way of declaring that his land, and his god, were superior to anything he would find down here.

Nevertheless, Naaman has made the journey from Damascus to Israel – the same road, most likely, used by Saul of Tarsus in the opposite direction just before his con-version. It's not a long journey: forty miles or so across the Golan Heights, which is still disputed territory nearly three thousand years later. It still has villages that change hands every time there's another war, and people, like Naaman's wife's servant-girl, who wake up to find themselves on the other side. But when Naaman travels to another country, it is normally at the head of a conquering army; and now here he is, a five-star general covered in medals, coming to knock on the door of a Jewish prophet, to ask a favour. No ordinary favour, either: Naaman wants to be cured of his leprosy. His god Rimmon can't do anything about it. And his wife's servant-girl seems to think, for some reason, that there is someone in Israel who can.

But in order to understand what Elisha does to Naaman we have to take a step back in time. The river Jordan played a vital role in the founding story of Israel, the story of the Exodus. Israel was enslaved in Egypt, and God brought her out through the Red Sea. But Israel was then in the wilder-ness for forty years, ending up to the East of the Jordan, just north of the Dead Sea. And they entered the Promised

Land *through* the Jordan, marching solemnly across the dried-up river while the priests stood in the middle carrying the ark of the covenant. Joshua then took twelve men, one from each tribe of Israel, and made them set up twelve stones in the river where the priests had stood, and twelve stones taken from the river on the bank where they ended up.

The symbolism is obvious. This crossing of the Jordan was the defining moment for the twelve tribes of Israel. It made them who they were; and it made the Promised Land what it was. Their God, the God of exodus and covenant, had brought them through the Jordan and was giving them the land.

From that moment, the Israelites looked back to the Exodus, the wilderness, and the crossing of the Jordan, as the means by which their God had made them his people, had set them free, had given them a new identity. That didn't make them perfect, of course. There was still a long way to go, with many sorrows and puzzles and failures to come. Precisely because they were free, they were free to rebel; and God, in his covenant love to them, was obliged to respond by sending them out of the land again, off into exile. But even in exile they remained the people who had been defined by that moment at the Jordan; and the covenant love of God reached out, yearning after them, urging them to return and be truly his people again. The wilderness and the river form the sign of the healing, restoring love of Israel's God, Yahweh.

So we should not be surprised at what Elisha tells Naaman to do. Naaman is used to people bowing and scraping before him, and has an amusingly unfocused idea of what a prophet should do to heal him of his leprosy: 'I thought he would come out and stand – and – and – invoke Yahweh his god ['his' god, please note: Naaman is still regarding Yahweh as a minor foreign deity who happens to

specialize in leprosy] – and invoke his god by name – and
wave his hand over the place – and – well, and cure me!'
But Elisha is not about to do anything so unfocused. If
Naaman wants to be cured by Yahweh, he must learn who
Yahweh is: he is not just the tribal god of Israel, but the God
of all the earth, the healing, liberating God, the God of creation and covenant, of Exodus, wilderness and Jordan, the
God of steadfast redeeming love. In for a penny, in for a
pound: if you want to do business with Yahweh, you must
go down to the Jordan, and wash. If you want the covenant
blessings, you must accept the covenant sign.

It is perhaps that challenge which momentarily sends
Naaman off in a rage. But when his servants cool him down
he realizes that he has no choice. So he goes down and
immerses himself seven times in the Jordan, as Elisha had
told him to; and his flesh is restored like that of a little
child. He is clean. And now comes the punch-line of the
whole story. He returns with his retinue, and stands before
Elisha and confesses his new-found faith. 'Now I know', he
says, 'that there is no God in all the earth except in Israel.'
Naaman still has a long way to go. He has to return to
Damascus, outwardly conforming to the way things are
done there, but with his heart on fire because he has met
and been healed by the one true God of all the earth. He
has a new loyalty, and out of sheer gratitude he will find the
way to be true. He has been given a new identity. He has
been defined, for good, by that moment at the Jordan.

Joshua and Naaman together help us to understand, as
we come to the banks of the muddy river Jordan, the powerful symbolism which it carried for Israel for over a thousand
years. So we should not be surprised, either, when we read,
not only in the New Testament but in the Jewish historian
Josephus, of a Jewish prophet leading a renewal movement,
summoning people to come down into the wilderness and

there symbolically to re-enact the entry into the Promised Land, the crossing of the Jordan. He stood there, this wild man, dressed like Elijah or Elisha, urging people, as Elisha had urged Naaman, that they should wash in the Jordan and become new people, indeed *a* new people, the people with whom Israel's God was at last renewing the covenant. The name of this prophet was John. And, as he plunged people into the water, immersing them and bringing them up the other side, he was not offering simply a new Jewish rite of purification, which they would have to repeat every time they contracted some uncleanness. This was their defining moment. They now had a new identity. They were now the renewed, new covenant people of God, and had to learn what that meant in practice. They had experienced the new Exodus, and must now look for the new Joshua who would lead them into the Promised Land.

And of course, as John was baptizing, there came one from Galilee, whose name was Joshua: *Yeshua*, or in Greek *Iesous*, Jesus. And when he went down into the water and came up the other side, the Spirit descended on him, and God himself declared that this was his beloved Son. And just as the many streams of eastern Israel run down into the Jordan, so the many rich streams of Israel's history were channelled into that one moment. This was the moment that would ever after define the people of God. The new covenant people were to be known as Jesus' people. If you want to belong to the people of God, you must follow the beloved Son. As Moses handed on the torch to Joshua, to lead the people into the Promised Land, so now the new Joshua would take over from the last of the prophets. He then came into Galilee, saying 'The time is fulfilled, and the Kingdom of God is at hand.'

It thus came about that all the symbolism which the Jordan had carried for the people of Israel through a millennium and a half was contained within the act of baptism, the place where Christian pilgrimage really gets under way. However the living God meets you – whether, like Paul on the road to Damascus, it happens in a blinding flash, or whether, like many others in New Testament times and since, it comes creeping over you, with a strange warmth and joy and challenge that the living God is addressing you, calling you, loving you, forgiving you and commissioning you – the many ways in to personal faith are all summed up and made public in baptism. In New Testament terms, an unbaptized Christian is an anomaly to be rectified as soon as possible. Baptism says what John was saying, what Elisha was saying to Naaman: here, washed in this water, are the covenant people of the one true God.

Christian baptism, which still in New Testament times looked back to John and the Jordan, quickly came to focus more specifically on Jesus himself, and on his death and resurrection. One of the first-century meanings of the Greek word *baptizomai* was 'to be drowned'; and within twenty-five years of Jesus' crucifixion, Paul, writing both to the Colossians and to the Romans, could speak, as of something that was common knowledge in the Church, of baptism as a sharing not just in the new covenant community but in the dying and rising of Jesus. Without losing any of its Jewish connotations, the act of plunging someone under the water and bringing them up again the other side spoke powerfully of dying to the old life and coming through into a new one. This was the defining moment, that which gave people a new identity. The wilderness and the river, the cross and the empty tomb, form the sign of the healing love of the creator and covenant God. If you want the covenant blessings, you must accept the covenant sign.

If we see baptism in this way, as the defining moment at the formal beginning of Christian pilgrimage, we should be able to avoid some of the problems that have often been associated with it. Much modern Western thinking has been deeply suspicious of symbolism and symbolic actions, seeing them as mere mumbo-jumbo. Baptism is often regarded as a useless ritual, more to do with social convention than with living faith. This is perhaps an inevitable reaction to the view which has so emphasized the sacramental validity of the action as to make it appear almost magical, as though by splashing water on someone and mumbling a few words one could make them a Christian and save their soul for ever. That view, indeed, resulted in Western Europe in the last generation in a situation summed up by Cardinal Suenens, the charismatic Archbishop of Maline-Bruxelles, in a mission address in the Sheldonian Theatre, Oxford. To a packed audience, he declared, 'The world is full of baptized non-Christians.' Clearly there is a problem there which we can't simply wish away. In our generation, though, we are starting to be aware again of the power of symbolic actions; and the time is therefore ripe to reappropriate the glory and mystery of baptism. Sacraments are not sympathetic magic; but neither are they mere empty signs.

You cannot, then, turn away from the font like a latter-day Naaman and say, 'I might as well have a bath at home in comfort.' You must abandon your cultural pride, and submit to the humiliation of sharing the death of Jesus, so that you may now be defined by that moment, that action, and set out on the new path of resurrection life. If you want to do business with Jesus, you must go down to the Jordan, and wash. You must publicly and visibly share his dying and rising, and be defined by that event for the rest of your life.

This enables us to understand the meaning of baptism for those of us, myself included, who were baptized as infants and who cannot consciously remember the event. Baptism is a beginning, not an ending. It is the start of a pil-

grimage, not its conclusion. Think again of the children of
Israel. They looked back to the wilderness and the Jordan
as the moment when God had set them free, had given
them a new identity. That didn't make them perfect, any
more than baptism makes us perfect. Precisely because God
has set us free, we are free to rebel, to go our own way. We
are free, like the Prodigal Son, to go off into exile, to choose
a way of life which will lead us far from our Father's house.
But even in exile we remain people who have been defined
by that moment under the water. The death and resurrection
of Jesus, to which baptism points, function for us like the
twelve stones in the river, defining who we are. And the
covenant love of God in Christ reaches out, yearning after
us, urging us to return and be truly his people again. This
is the situation of someone who has been baptized as an
infant. They are who they are because of that moment; but,
precisely since they are defined as God's free children, they
are free to rebel.

Paul addresses just this situation frequently in his letters.
His hearers have been baptized; very well, they must now
work out in practice that to which baptism points. It is not
enough to say, 'Oh well, I've been baptized, so it doesn't
matter how I live or think now.' The very meaning of
baptism is precisely that you have set out on a pilgrim path,
following Jesus in the way of the cross. That is who you are,
by definition.

Putting off baptism until teenage years or adulthood
doesn't actually change this situation. Every baptized adult
will know times when following Jesus is the last thing they
want to do, when their one desire is to rebel, risking or
perhaps deliberately courting exile, the response of the
covenant God to covenant disobedience. Paul regularly appeals
for faith and obedience *on the basis of* baptism. You have
started on the pilgrim road, he says; you have been defined,

in baptism, by the death and resurrection of Jesus. Now you must go on.

Paul also insists that baptism, in defining us as the renewed people of God in Christ, is the only definition that matters. We are constantly tempted to define ourselves in other ways: to demarcate our identity in terms of social status, gender, age, wealth (or lack of it), class, nationality or race; but under the water all these things cease to matter. Listen to what Paul says in Galatians 3, taking the words which God spoke to Jesus at his baptism and applying them to all of us:

> You are all children of God, through faith, in Christ Jesus; for all of you who were baptized into Christ have put on Christ. There is neither Jew nor Greek, slave nor free, male and female, for you are all one in Christ Jesus.

Baptism is our common beginning. It defines us as the covenant family of the one true God. With every eucharist, as we say the Creed, we repeat the words that were spoken at our baptism, when, like Naaman coming up out of the water and finding himself cured, we declare that there is no God in all the earth except this one. And then, as we feast together at the family table, we discover that the God who called us into pilgrimage, and defined us as his sons and daughters in the waters of baptism, signifying our sharing in the death and resurrection of Jesus, now gives us the appropriate food to strengthen us on our way. As we enter upon our pilgrimage, we remind ourselves of what happened at the Jordan, and to us at the font, in order to remind ourselves of who God truly is, and of who we really are. The water, the bread and the wine speak volumes; they are true signposts. This is indeed the way to the Promised Land.

THREE

The Way of the Wilderness

THE ROAD FROM the Jordan to Jerusalem lies through the desert.

A wise old Jewish writer, about two hundred years before the time of Jesus, put it like this: 'My child, if you come to serve the Lord, prepare yourself for temptation.' Or, as the Gospel writers might see it, after their description of Jesus at his baptism: 'If you really are filled with the Spirit, you should expect to be led into the wilderness.'

You are never far from the wilderness when you're in the Promised Land. Just a few miles to the south or south-east, or to the north-east across the Jordan, and you're out in the desert. When the Israeli soldiers go into that desert, they drink a pint of water every hour just to stay healthy. From the top of the Mount of Olives itself you look west over Jerusalem itself, with its vines and fig trees and other signs of fertile life, and east down to the Dead Sea; and between you and the Dead Sea there is desert, wilderness. The rain comes up from the Mediterranean, falling on the hills of Judaea up to and including Jerusalem and the Mount of Olives. From there on eastwards it's all dry, except for the occasional storm that sends flash floods down the wadis to the Dead Sea. When you're in Jerusalem, the wilderness is just over the next hill.

From at least the time of the letter to the Hebrews, the wilderness has been used in Christian writing as an image for the dark side of the spiritual journey. Conversion, baptism, faith – a rich sense of the presence and love of God, of vocation and sonship; and then, the wilderness. If you come to serve the Lord, get ready for the temptation. If you want to go from the Jordan to Jerusalem, get your desert boots on. Nor is this simply like saying that if you want to learn to play Mozart you will have to practise your scales, or that if you want to speak German you will have to learn your irregular verbs. That's part of it, but it's much deeper. Christian writers of all sorts, throughout the centuries, have insisted that it is part, a necessary part it seems, of the Christian pilgrimage that at some stage, perhaps at several stages, we shall be called to travel through the wilderness:

In order to arrive at what you do not know
  You must go by a way which is the way of ignorance.
In order to possess what you do not possess
  You must go by the way of dispossession.
In order to arrive at what you are not
  You must go through the way in which you are not.

The wilderness comes in many shapes and sizes, just as the deserts of Judaea and Sinai are by no means uniform. I used to think of deserts as simply miles and miles of flat sands, punctuated by the odd oasis; but the wilderness that surrounds the Promised Land comes in many forms. There are huge crags, like Masada, the last bastion of the revolutionaries after the fall of Jerusalem, an enormous barren rock to the south-west of the Dead Sea. There are gullies and crevasses, great rocky outcrops and hidden valleys. Walk a mile or two off the road and you could get lost quite easily.

The wilderness of the spiritual journey is much like that. For some, it is simply a sense that everything has gone very dry. There is no delight in prayer or reading the scriptures. Going to church has become boring and futile. The sacraments seem a pointless ritual. Where before there was a sense of God's presence as a loving parent, gently nursing and guiding, or of the wise prompting of the Holy Spirit, there now seems to be a great emptiness. The story of Jesus, once so full of interest and stimulation, the scrap-book of the life of a new best friend, seems dull, and even the story of the cross and resurrection has apparently lost its power to sweep the heart. This is the common experience of many, many Christians at some stage in their pilgrimage. Tragically, some at once conclude that what happened at the Jordan was all a delusion, a passing phase, that there really is no Jerusalem to go on to. Others wander blindly without hope, and stumble by accident – or was it an accident? – back on to the right path. But the way of Christian maturity is to recognize the desert path for what it is – another mile on the road called 'Faithfulness' – and to tread it with obedience and patience:

I said to my soul, be still, and wait without hope
For hope would be hope for the wrong thing; wait
    without love
For love would be love of the wrong thing; there is
    yet faith
But the faith and the love and the hope are all in
    the waiting.
Wait without thought, for you are not ready for thought:
So the darkness shall be the light, and the stillness
    the dancing.

Of course, there are many obvious factors that can contribute to this sense of desolation, of wilderness. It is never what we would call, perhaps misleadingly, a 'purely spiritual' thing. Tiredness can contribute a good deal to it. When Elijah was fleeing from Jezebel after killing the prophets of Baal, he went off into the wilderness a day's journey, and was so depressed he asked God to kill him then and there. What was God's answer? Many things; but the first three were sleep, food and drink, twice over. Only then was Elijah ready for the next leg of his wilderness journey.

Sometimes this whole sequence can be self-caused. We allow pressure to mount up; we persuade ourselves we haven't got time to rest, or we don't eat properly because we're working too hard; the messages of protest our bodies send us don't get through, and eventually the system shuts down. If, in that condition, we mistake a symptom of the problem – our inability to sense the presence and love of God – for the root cause, we are in danger of cosmic projection, of blaming God for our own problem, like a child locking himself in a room and then shouting angrily at his mother for not coming in to find him.

But sometimes the problem is simply unavoidable. It may have medical roots, like the tiredness and depression that often follow an operation or the birth of a child. Sometimes it may be in our immediate and unavoidable circumstances, as we watch someone very close to us succumb to a life-threatening disease. Sometimes it may be the natural effect of a major change in life: a new job, moving to a new area, a change in family circumstances. The lines of interconnection between the mental, the physical, the emotional and the spiritual are far more subtle and complex than we normally suppose; and if you think you can perform on one of those levels only while leaving the others unaffected, you've probably got another think coming. One way or another, the result is often a time in the wilderness. It isn't far away; it's just over the hill.

In particular, of course, the wilderness is the place of

temptation. It's the place where the real choices are made. It's one thing to go with the crowd, down to the Jordan for baptism or into the Holy City chanting Hosanna. But when you're on your own, and it's hot and dusty and lonely and you're not sure quite where you are: who are you? What's it all about anyway? Why not . . . turn these stones into bread? Did God really say 'You are my beloved child, with you I am well pleased?' Was it all a dream? If God really meant it, why are you feeling like this now? Why not turn aside, and avail yourself of the same pleasures and thrills that everyone else has? It isn't natural, you know, all this fasting and praying. You need to live in the real world and stop fooling yourself.

And when the more obvious temptations have been dealt with, the bigger, more subtle ones move in on us, as they did on Jesus. Pride and power – as long as you sell your soul. Experiment with God's power and love – put God to the test – and see what you can get away with. Temptations are often hard to recognize because they are distortions of a true vocation. God had intended that Jesus should be set in authority over the world, to use his God-given power to bring in the kingdom; but not like this, by satisfying his own hunger or performing circus stunts. To distinguish between vocation and temptation demands for us, as it did for Jesus, real clarity about our own calling. And which of us is ever fully clear about that?

In fact, one of the truly frightening things about the wilderness is how many voices you hear out there. When you turn off the TV and the radio and the portable stereo and walk away from the chatter and the busyness of ordinary life, and in the silence start to listen (and if that sounds like a novel experience, I suggest it is overdue), what do you hear? And what do you make of what you hear? Do you listen uncritically and go with the flow? Or do you make the hard decision to sift and sort the voices, learning to listen for the voice of God, whether it be the voice of comfort or the voice of vocation, and learning to recognize the voice which sounds so plausible, so reasonable, such a relief indeed, but which is actually the voice that distorts God's call, that distracts from God's way, that will lead us round and round in circles in the wilderness and abandon us with a mocking laugh? Get ready for the wilderness. If you have begun your pilgrimage, sooner or later you will find it, or it will find you. And if you are there right now, take comfort. It is part of the deal.

That is the first, and in some ways the most important thing to be said in this chapter. And the second grows out of it. The wilderness is not simply an area through which the pilgrim way unfortunately happens to pass. The wilderness is the place where we are to learn new things about ourselves and about God. And sometimes the right questions to ask, when we find ourselves in the wilderness, are not 'Why?' or 'Why me?' – questions to which we may well not find an answer, or not for some years. Nor is the right question 'When?' – when will this be over, so that I can resume something like normality? The right questions to ask may well be 'What?' What am I supposed to make of this? What can I do with this? And 'Who?' Who do I discover myself to be in the wilderness? And, even more important, who do I discover God to be?

Much of our culture seems designed to prevent us from even asking these questions. The pace at which we live, the noise with which we surround ourselves, and the paperwork we generate and smother one another with, all have the effect of preventing us from stopping for a moment or two to take stock, to ask who we are, who God is, and what might this thing be that he and I have going between us. Sometimes the wilderness is God's way of stripping away all the surrounding noise and happy or unhappy confusion, so that we can face, before it's too late, the questions we know, deep down, that we really must face. This, perhaps, is the reason why the letter to the Hebrews, at the end of its long discussion of the wilderness wanderings of the people of God, warns in chapter 4 that before God no creature is hidden: all are naked and laid bare to the eyes of the one with whom we have to do. And it is in the light of that that the writer goes on to point to Jesus, who has been in the wilderness ahead of us, and now comes alongside us to comfort us when we find ourselves there.

What the wilderness does, of course – whether it is depression or temptation, suffering or persecution (I have not spoken of persecution yet, but we should not forget that millions of our brothers and sisters in various parts of the world worship God in Christ in fear of their lives, at risk of beatings, torture, rape, slavery and death, either sudden or lingering; their wilderness is starker and more obvious than ours) – is to expose us to things that are going on inside us as well as outside. That is why, of course, the geographical desert is so compelling, so evocative. The wilderness around us opens our eyes, if we let it, to the wilderness within. If that were not so, we could go on our way from Jordan to Jerusalem without the wilderness getting to us.

No: there is a bit of 'us' within that corresponds to the wilderness without. A bit of chaos, a dry waste long in need of irrigation, a bit where the wind blows dust into your eyes, where you feel you are probably lost but you are too tired to work out why. The time in the wilderness is the time when we should be honest about the wilderness within: when we should look at the chaos we have been trying to ignore, find water to pour on the thirsty ground, clear the dust from our eyes, and see the way clear ahead once more. Just as many of us have a room in the house where we dump things we don't know what to do with, while knowing in our heart of hearts we shall have to sort it all out some day, so most of us have at least locked cupboards in our inner worlds where there's a lot of junk we can't get rid of but would much rather not sort out just now. The problem, as we all know, is that if we don't sort it out, things spill out from time to time, and sooner or later the cupboard door may burst open altogether. One of the reasons God brings us into the wilderness is that he longs for us to be more integrated, more in tune with our whole selves. That is often a dry and dusty job, and we will wish with all our hearts we didn't have to do it.

Equally important, if not more so, the wilderness experience can open our ears to hear the pain of the world. When we are trundling along quite content with our lot, it is easy to ignore the cries for help that come from the rest of the world: from our fellow-Christians who still today suffer systematic major persecution; from orphans, refugees, widows and homeless people of all faiths and none; from the homeless and alienated within our own society, not least our inner cities; and from those who day by day carry a load of pain that bows them down inside even though nobody seems to notice. As we learn to listen to the sounds of the wilderness, including the pain that bubbles up from our own hearts, we learn to listen, too, to the pain of the world. God does not want cheerful, shallow, flippant and easy-going pilgrims to arrive in Jerusalem with their hands in their pockets, casually whistling a psalm. He wants them to arrive in his presence bringing with them the pain of the world, so that the tears of the desert may be presented in his Temple, before the throne of grace.

If we are open to this dimension of the wilderness experience, we may begin to discover what we would never have otherwise expected: that the one true and living God is also the God of the wilderness. That, indeed, is part of the point of the story of Jesus' temptations. God's beloved Son spends forty days in the wilderness, tempted as we are, yet without sin; he is therefore a high priest who is able to sympathize with our weaknesses. He has trodden the pilgrim path ahead of us. Hidden within that story we discover what the children of Israel discovered, what Elijah discovered, that the living God is hiding in the wilderness, waiting to be discovered afresh, waiting to meet us in a new way, a way marked to be sure with the sign of the cross, but a way of new intimacy, new depths that only the silence and dust of the wilderness could make space for. This is, after all, why the Desert Fathers were the Desert Fathers: not because they were escaping from the wicked ways of the cities (they knew, none better, that even the saint carries wickedness into the desert with him), but because they knew that in the desert God was to be found in a fresh way.

That is, after all, the biblical message. When God is faced with the infidelity of his bride Israel, he plans to woo her back to himself. Where will he do this? Why, in the wilderness, of course, the place where the covenant was made at the first. He takes her back to the place where they fell in love: 'I will allure her, and bring her into the wilderness, and speak to her heart' (Hosea 2.14). And it is because of this that several psalms begin in the wilderness and end with shouts of praise. 'My soul thirsts for you, my flesh faints for you, as in a dry and barren land where no water is' (Psalm 63.2) is swiftly followed by 'My soul is satisfied as with marrow and fatness, and my mouth praises you with joyful lips.' Those who faithfully follow the pilgrim way through the wilderness will find, sooner or later – and it may well be much later – that the God they never really

knew was there all along, and that in discovering the depths
within their own hearts they were discovering the depths of
the heart of God.

It is only then that we dare to listen to the words of
promise that the wilderness experience had all but obliter-
ated. When we open ourselves to walk the desert path to
which God has called us – when we accept it with humility,
with patience and with obedient hope – then we hear again
the words we had almost forgotten, which speak of Easter
seen through the cross, still no doubt a long way off, but
still God's true promise:

> The wilderness and the barren land shall be
>   glad and rejoice;
> the desert shall rejoice and blossom.
>
> . . .
>
> they shall see the glory of the Lord,
> the majesty of our God.
>
> . . .
>
> Then shall the eyes of the blind be opened,
> and the ears of the deaf unstopped;
> then shall the lame leap like a deer
> and the tongue of the dumb sing for joy;
> for waters shall break forth in the wilderness,
> and streams in the desert.
>
> . . .
>
> And the ransomed of the Lord shall return
> and come to Zion with singing;
>
> . . .
>
> they shall receive joy and gladness,
> and sorrow and sighing shall flee away. (Isaiah 35)

FOUR

The Way to Galilee

> O Sabbath rest by Galilee
> O calm of hills above;
> Where Jesus knelt to share with thee
> The silence of eternity
> Interpreted by love.

A FAVOURITE VERSE from a favourite hymn – certainly one
of my lifelong favourites. And when you go to Galilee today
on pilgrimage that verse seems to be reinforced. Unless you
are unlucky with the weather, Galilee seems to exude peace
and tranquillity. The gentle lapping of the waters of the
lake, the hills rising up like a softer version of the English
Lake District, the whisper of the wind in the reeds, the
rural landscape at peace all around: all of this seems to
underline the message that Jesus' Galilean ministry was a
time when he enjoyed the peace of God embodied in his
native countryside, and invited others to share it too.

And then we read the Gospels again, and we find things
weren't quite so simple, or so silent. Take a passage like
Matthew 12. Here we are, at the heart of Jesus' Galilean
ministry. Jesus' agenda and activity is felt by the self-
appointed guardians of Israel's traditions to be so threatening that they declare he is in league with the Devil; and
Jesus issues a stern announcement that the kingdom of
God, breaking into the life of Galilee, is not so much an

invitation to go on a retreat in a romantic landscape but a summons to join in with the work of plundering the strong man's house, now that the strong man has been tied up.

Now of course there is plenty of evidence that Jesus appreciated the delicate beauty of the Galilean countryside. He spoke feelingly of the lilies of the field, the birds of the air, of the Father's concern for a single fallen sparrow, of seed-time and harvest, and of the rain and sunshine as the evidence of the creator's care for his whole world. Jesus cannot have been unaware that the Galilee where he grew up was, as it still is, a remarkably fertile place, blessed with unique climatic conditions that enable plants of all sorts to grow side by side, well watered and very fruitful. It was not simply a dream when he spoke of crops springing up, some thirty, some sixty, and some a hundredfold. Jesus clearly had a ready eye to see illustrations and parables in the natural world, as the great Hebrew prophets had before him. His native Galilee was indeed, and can be for us as we visit it on pilgrimage, a glorious and many-sided reminder of the goodness of the creator God.

But Jesus' Galilee was far from tranquil. Most people, Jesus probably included, didn't have much time or energy to wander dreamily in the hills like some Lake District poet born eighteen centuries too soon. For three hundred years already by Jesus' time, Galilee had been 'Galilee of the Gentiles', surrounded to the north and east by pagan city-states, which over time had spread the tentacles of pagan culture deep into the heart of Galilee itself. To the south there lay Samaria, comprising much of what we today call the West Bank, separating Galilean Jews from their fellow-Jews in Judaea and Jerusalem. Then, as now, there was deep mutual distrust and hatred between the inhabitants of Judaea and Galilee on the one hand and those of Samaria on the other. Galilee remained Jewish territory, but there was no invisible protective curtain to keep foreign ideas out. There were many places in Jesus' native Galilee where you would find pagan towns, with their theatres, temples, and idols. Since Galilee was very fertile and well situated on the trade routes, it was quite a rich plum for whoever happened to gain power there. And in Jesus' day that meant, of course, the house of Herod.

Herod the Great had been granted the title of King of the Jews by the Romans roughly forty years before Jesus was born. He wasn't of royal blood; he just happened to be the most effective thug around. Herod's rule was bloodstained and effective. When he met resistance, as he often did, he simply sent the troops in. When he suspected rival claims to his throne, not least from within his own family, he acted with increasing paranoia and brutality. The riches produced by fertile Galilee did not, for the most part, find their way in an equitable fashion into the homes and pockets of those who worked on the land. They sustained Herod and his court in an increasingly luxurious lifestyle, with lavish palaces and fortresses. When Herod the Great died, just after Jesus of Nazareth was born, his kingdom was divided between his three sons; and Galilee fell to Herod Antipas, the Herod we meet in the Gospel stories, the Herod who was challenged by Jesus' cousin John the Baptist, the Herod whose daughter demanded, and got, John's head.

That, I am afraid, was the Galilee that Jesus lived in, rather than the romantic watercolour scene. Oh, and the hills above the lake were not exactly calm, either; they provided places where the holy brigands would hide out, longing for revolution, for God's kingdom to come and sweep away the Herods of this world, and the Caesars too, for that matter.

The significance of Galilee within Jesus' ministry, then, is not first and foremost that it is an evocative place within which to develop a life of tranquil spirituality. That may or may not be the effect it has on us today. Galilee is the kingdom-place. It is where Jesus begins his announcement of the kingdom of God.

One of the reasons why the romantic view of Galilee has taken such a firm hold in much Christian imagination is that Christian tradition has not really known what to do with the public ministry of Jesus. The great creeds of the Church jump straight from Jesus' birth to his death, implying that all the stuff in between was of less importance. The Litany in the old Anglican Prayer Book, invoking what it saw as the key events of Jesus' life, got slightly further but not much: first we say 'By the mystery of thy holy Incarnation; by thy holy Nativity and Circumcision; by thy Baptism, Fasting and Temptation'; and then we go straight on to 'By thine Agony and bloody Sweat; by the Cross and Passion; by thy precious Death and Burial; by the glorious Resurrection and Ascension; and by the coming of the Holy Ghost'. That adds the temptation, and Gethsemane, to the picture we get in the creeds, but it still leaves a large void in the middle.

The shaping of the traditional Christian year gives much the same impression: Christmas, Epiphany, Candlemas, and then Lent, which, as it has now developed, draws together precisely the forty days in the wilderness and the time of the passion. None of these schemes begin to do justice to what the Gospel writers tell us on page after page: that Jesus came into Galilee announcing God's kingdom. The traditional ways of telling the story have left a vacuum, a hole in the middle of the narrative, which different generations have filled in different ways, the Victorians not least by sentimentalizing the picture of Jesus in Galilee, and implying that it was a time of sweetness and light, of gentle Jesus meek and mild, of sabbath rests by Galilee and calm of hills above.

It is therefore time that we rehabilitate, in our patterns of spirituality as well as in our thinking, a sense of what Jesus' Galilean ministry was all about. Some newer litanies, in various recent publications, add a thoroughly appropriate and necessary clause, bridging the gap between Jesus' wilderness temptations and his passion: 'By your ministry in word and work; by your mighty acts of power; and by your preaching of the kingdom'. It is on that Galilean spirituality, based on God's power breaking in to the world through the words and deeds of Jesus, that we must now focus as the next step of our pilgrimage.

Jesus' announcement of God's kingdom burst into the middle of rival visions of what kingdom in general, and God's kingdom in particular, might mean. Herod's kingdom, luxurious in itself and brutal in its effects, was bitterly resented by his orthodox Jewish subjects on both grounds, but more particularly because of Herod's many compromises with paganism. And the Galilean Jews, whom archaeology reveals to have been mostly devout and orthodox, became more and more frustrated with Herod's rule, and the Roman overlordship upon which it was based. They longed for God to become king, and were increasingly prepared to use any means available, including violence, to bring this goal about. They had their own kingdom-agenda, their own kingdom-movement; and they believed it was what God commanded. Galilee was not the only place where revolution was in the air, but the hills above the lake were busy with it. And the sabbath rest by Galilee was not a delightful Victorian Sunday of leisurely spiritual reflection, but a jealously guarded cultural symbol, which said 'We sabbath-keepers are the true people of God, and sabbath-breakers are compromising with the enemy.'

It is that alternative kingdom-agenda which explains the otherwise astonishing hostility of the Pharisees to Jesus in some Gospel passages. What's wrong with Jesus healing someone who is dumb, blind and demon-possessed? Nothing in itself; but Jesus had acquired a reputation in Galilee, a reputation for doing things upside down and inside out, a reputation for healing on the sabbath, for challenging conventions, for starting a different sort of kingdom-movement. His parables confronted existing views of the kingdom with a new one, in which God's power and love would come to reign not by revolutionary violence but by the way of the cross. He was already perceived to be subversive. And when someone like that does mighty acts of healing, the onlookers are faced with a choice. Either this is the work of God, validating Jesus' whole kingdom-agenda; or we shall have to explain it some other way. If it is not from God, such activity must be the work of Satan.

This charge draws out of Jesus a key statement about his own work. He is not an emissary of the prince of darkness. On the contrary, the fact that he casts out demons by the Spirit of God shows that Satan's kingdom is shaken to its core; that God's way of establishing his rule is being put into effect through his (Jesus') work. Jesus has won the battle in the wilderness, the battle with the oldest enemy; now he comes into Galilee putting that victory into effect. How can one plunder the strong man's house unless you first tie up the strong man? Then indeed you may plunder his house. Jesus' exorcisms are therefore signs that he has won the initial victory, that Satan's kingdom is indeed under serious threat.

This claim creates an inevitable division within his onlookers. Whoever is not with me is against me; whoever does not gather with me scatters. If you look at the work of God and declare it to be the work of the Devil, then you have painted yourself into a corner from which there is no escape. You have denied the one hope of rescue. You have cut off the last branch that was safe to sit on. This Galilean kingdom-message is anything but a recipe for a quiet life, a passive or romantic spirituality. It is an invitation to a kingdom-spirituality, invoking the power of the king to liberate those held in Satan's bondage. Jesus has a certain amount to say about Herod and his kingdom; about Caesar, too, and his. But the real rival kingdom to God's kingdom is Satan. Herod and Caesar are no doubt in their own ways agents of Satan, with their greedy and brutal regimes, but Satan is just as pleased when people take it upon themselves to oppose Caesar and Herod with the pagan, satanic means of violent revolution. 'Pride of man and earthly glory', says the hymn, 'sword and crown betray his trust'. Jesus comes without a sword, without a crown, but with the power and the victory of God.

Now do you see what you lose if you base your spirituality on a story of Jesus which jumps straight from Bethlehem to Calvary, or from the wilderness to Gethsemane? Once you sign on for pilgrimage, in baptism and conversion, you commit yourself, not only to periodic sojourning in the wilderness, as we were thinking in the last chapter, but also to the Galilean battle for the kingdom. You commit yourself to deeds and words which say, as Jesus' deeds and words did, that there is another king, that there is another way of organizing the world than the way of Caesar and Herod, that there is another kingdom than the kingdom of swords and crowns. You commit yourself to the work of healing and liberation, both actual and symbolic. You commit yourself to freeing slaves, to loosening the bonds of debt, to bringing good news to the poor. And you commit yourself to doing those things, not as a grand social action which you will implement by your own energy and ingenuity, but in the power, and with the weapons, of the kingdom of God: by prayer and fasting, by truth and righteousness, by the gospel of peace, by faith, by salvation, by the word of God.

Those, indeed, are the weapons which Paul describes when he paints his picture of the kingdom-warrior in Ephesians 6. And your pilgrimage must include this kingdom-work at every level: in your voting and in your marriage; in your politics and in your office; in your cheque-book and in your social life. And, of course, in your worship and Christian fellowship. If it is true that in Jesus the Galilean the living God has fought and won the battle for the kingdom – and if that isn't true we are wasting our time in even thinking about him and his life – then the task of those who follow his pilgrim way must inevitably be to plant the flag of the kingdom in territory at present occupied by other contesting claimants.

Where do you begin this task? There are at least three possible answers, and it doesn't much matter which you take as long as you then move on to the other one as well.

Some find a burning need to begin their kingdom-task by challenging injustice and oppression in the wider world. That is a vital and non-negotiable aspect of Christian work. How we go about it is of course a matter of debate and discernment. That we must go about it is part of the deal. It comes with the territory – with the territory, so to speak, of Galilee. That's no bad place to start.

Some find that their chief desire as Christians is to create beauty and truth through art, or music, or scholarship, so that the beauty and truth of God may shine into the ugliness and untruth of the world. That, too, is a vital and God-given part of kingdom-work. It, too, goes with the territory. It is part of the battle: speak the truth and shame the Devil.

Others find that their initial Christian vocation is to challenge the contesting claimants in their own heart and life. When they hear the gospel message they realize just how far they have fallen short, how much they are blind to the things of God, and dumb to speak his word; and they find themselves called to a holiness of life, a struggle against sin within themselves, planting the flag of the kingdom in their own daily words and deeds. That too, I suggest, comes with the territory. It is no bad place to start. People often use the season of Lent as a time for special reflection and renewed effort along these lines. We can even reclaim parts of that old hymn: 'Reclothe us in our rightful mind, in purer lives thy service find, in deeper reverence praise.'

But whichever place you start, make sure you go on to the others. Break into the circle of holiness somewhere, it doesn't matter where, and continue right around it. Don't use a strong social concern as an excuse for not facing up to the personal battles that you have to fight; don't fall in love with your own creativity so strongly that you lose sight of the call to justice and holiness; equally, don't get so focused on your private holiness that you forget God's passion for justice and truth, his compassion for the widow, orphan and oppressed, his passion and compassion which came together in the person of Jesus, which blossomed and flowered and bore fruit in the fertile soil of Galilee, and which went to Jerusalem to be enthroned. This is true kingdom-spirituality, Galilee-spirituality if you like. The Son of God was revealed, says St John, that he might destroy the works of the Devil. We who celebrate his victory are required, in our pilgrimage, to implement it.

> Pride of man and earthly glory,
> Sword and crown betray his trust;
> What with care and toil he buildeth,
> Tower and temple, fall to dust.
> But God's power, hour by hour
> Is my temple and my tower.

FIVE

The Way to Jerusalem

THE WAY TO Jerusalem is paved with great expectations.

Jerusalem, after all, is the city of the great king, the joy of the whole earth. It is Jerusalem the golden, with milk and honey blest. It is the place where the living God has chosen to put his name: 'Zion is my dwelling, my abode for all generations.' It is the city where David built his own house and then planned God's house. It is the city towards which Daniel in Babylon kept his window open in prayer, even at the risk of his life. Abraham passed by here, on his first journey into the land of promise; according to legend, Zion is the mountain where Abraham took Isaac to offer him in sacrifice. In other legends, it is the place where Adam and Eve themselves were buried. It is the city of dreams, the Holy City, the ultimate place of pilgrimage. It was and is a city of breathtaking beauty, high up in the Judaean mountains, encompassing in itself steep hills and deep gullies, with stunning views and gorgeous buildings, honeycombed with twisting alleyways, shafts of sunlight into beautiful courtyards, full of the smells of spices and olives, fresh bread and sweet wine, and of the sounds of many languages, many voices raised in prayer, many cocks crowing.

It is also the place of great pain. David captured Jerusalem from the Jebusites, about three thousand years ago; the current Israeli celebrations of Jerusalem's 3,000th anniversary are blatant propaganda, since there was already a city, belonging to the inhabitants of the land, and David took it by force. Since then, Jerusalem has been besieged, destroyed, rebuilt, destroyed again, rebuilt, besieged, fought over, again and again. As I prepare this text for publication, in June 1998, news arrives of yet another contentious and dangerous political move in and around the city. Jerusalem is to this day a city filled with enormous tensions, as the fragile settlement under the last mayor, Teddy Kolleck, in which Israelis and Palestinians were given a chance to live side by side, has given way to a new regime in which militant Israelis, intending to possess the whole place, are steadily ousting Palestinians from their two-thousand-year-old homes, forgetting perhaps that they too are children of Abraham. From the Anglican cathedral, St George's, where I lived for three months in 1989, you can walk two minutes into the main street of Palestinian East Jerusalem, where the tensions and the anger of fifty years of occupation and harassment can be felt in the air; or you can walk seven minutes the other way into Mea Shearim, the ultra-orthodox Jewish quarter, where the atmosphere is dominated by memories of Adolf Hitler and longings for the Messiah.

The joy of the world and the pain of the world, side by side and somehow intermingling. 'We are going up to Jerusalem,' said Jesus, 'and the Son of Man will be handed over to suffering and death.' The message they wanted to hear, and the message they didn't want to hear. They come together. Great expectations, containing and perhaps concealing great affliction.

In Jewish history and scripture, there were two reasons in particular for going to Jerusalem. You went there to enthrone the king, or to pay him homage. And you went there to meet God, to offer sacrifice, to celebrate his love, his salvation, his covenant. It was never quite that easy, of course. All kings have their opponents; often, to be near the king was to be in the danger zone. And the way into the presence of God remained dark and mysterious, assisted and sometimes blocked by priests, illuminated and sometimes obscured by prophets. And for long periods of Jewish history, ancient and modern, it was rumoured that God had abandoned Zion, at least temporarily, so that what was left was a strong memory, like the warmth in a bed where someone has been sleeping but isn't any more.

Enthroning the king and meeting God. Jerusalem is the natural royal seat; it is the natural place of worship. Jesus, up there in northern Galilee, was inviting his followers to join him in that double pilgrimage, with its multiple ambiguities. And to make this invitation he took them to Caesarea Philippi (Matthew 16.13–20).

There are, predictably, many towns called Caesarea scattered around the Roman empire, just as Alexander the Great left a trail of Alexandrias in the broad wake of his conquests. Caesarea Philippi lies on the slopes of Mount Hermon, at the source of the river Jordan, at the extreme north of the Holy Land. It's roughly twenty miles north of the Sea of Galilee, and only about forty miles south-west of Damascus, in Syria. Looking south from there, the whole of the land stretches out before you, and you can see in your mind's eye the great city, Jerusalem itself, nearly a hundred miles to the south.

To many Galileans of Jesus' day, Jerusalem represented the place both of hope and of frustration. It remained the place of pilgrimage and prayer, the place to which one day God would return in glory and victory, but at the moment it was the place where the wicked regime of the current chief priests held sway, ruling as puppets under the Roman governor, a hated pseudo-aristocracy, feathering their own nests, using their religious position to bolster and buffer their political status. Many a Galilean in Jesus' day, planning a pilgrimage to Jerusalem, would not only sing the Psalms of Ascent ('I was glad when they said unto me "We will go into the house of the Lord"'), but would also cherish the dream that one day they would go there in the company of the Messiah, who would sweep away the wicked rulers, priests, Herods, Romans, the lot, and who would reign as God's anointed one, in justice and peace. Great, and risky, expectations.

And now at last these twelve men believe this is the moment. Jesus has led them about Galilee doing extraordinary things, teaching about God's kingdom. The crowds are puzzled by him. 'Who do people say that the Son of Man is?' They think he's a prophet: maybe he's John the Baptist, maybe he's Elijah or Jeremiah, one of the great prophets of old. 'But who do you say that I am?' Pause, hush, and cue for Peter to speak for them all. 'You're the king,' he says. 'You're God's anointed. You're the son of the living God.'

No, he didn't mean 'You're the second person of the Trinity.' 'Son of God' was and is a Jewish title for great David's greater son, and it was only after the resurrection that a deeper truth, hidden within the old biblical language, began to dawn on Jesus' joyful but puzzled followers. And Jesus solemnly blesses Peter: the recognition that he, Jesus, is the Messiah could not have been deduced from current Jewish expectations, but only as a gift of recognition from the Father. Then comes the great promise: on this rock I shall build my church, and the gates of hell shall not prevail against it.

Some think, and the more I reflect on it the more I am inclined to agree, that this is a deliberate coded challenge to Jerusalem. Jerusalem is the city built on the rock, with the Temple within it as the house built on the rock. Jesus has already said, in the Sermon on the Mount, that to build your house anywhere other than the rock of his kingdom-message is to court disaster (Matthew 7.24–7). Now he greets Peter's announcement of his Messiahship as the rock on which his own house will be built, and the great, and now evil, city a hundred miles to the south will tremble at the thought of it. For now, we must keep this secret; don't tell anyone about this dream of Messiahship; but, of course, we are now planning to go to Jerusalem. Our preliminary days in Galilee are over. It's time to head south. Jerusalem is where kings go to get enthroned. This, of course, is precisely the message they wanted to hear. Their expectations, already high, are now at bursting point. They are ready to go. They are ready to enthrone Jesus as king: king of the Jews, king of the world.

But they are not ready for the sort of enthronement Jesus has in mind. When the Son of Man goes to Jerusalem he must suffer many things at the hands of the elders and chief priests and scribes, and be killed, and on the third day be raised. They are not ready to see their hopes crucified. They are not ready to see their expectations turned upside down and inside out in order to be fulfilled. They want the kingdom of God the way they've always wanted it, thank you very much. Oh, they've expected it'll be tough, but they're ready for that. Jesus' challenge about taking up the cross – stark as it must have been in that country where crosses, and what happened to people on them, were all too well known – is readily interpreted as exactly the sort of challenge people like Peter are eager to meet. It's going to be hard. You may have to suffer. You're not going to like it. Fine; all the more glory when we eventually come through.

They don't, perhaps, penetrate to the innermost meaning of the challenge. If anyone wants to come after me, let him deny himself, and take up his cross; for anyone who wants to save his life will lose it, and those who lose their life for my sake will find it. What will it profit someone to gain the whole world, but forfeit their life, their soul, their heart?

Yes, the kingdom is coming, and sooner than you think. Your expectations will be more than fulfilled. But the only way for that to happen is for them first to be dashed to pieces, broken in fragments on the dusty floor, so that God can make a new jigsaw out of them, one that conforms to his sort of kingdom. Part of the paradox of the Gospel story is that Jesus' closest followers, who understood him best, had their own ways of deeply misunderstanding him. Jesus was indeed going up to Jerusalem to become king. But his throne would not be the conventional sort. When, later on, two of his followers on the road to Jerusalem requested that they be allowed to sit one on his right and one on his left when he was enthroned as king, Jesus told them that they didn't know what they were talking about (Matthew 20.20–3). Skilled craftsmen take months to make a conventional royal throne; it took the soldiers only a few minutes to construct one for Jesus.

When we think of Peter with his blustering confidence, his attempt to order Jesus about, we are bound to think also of a cock crowing in the early spring morning near the governor's palace in Jerusalem. And we then learn – and perhaps this is part of the lesson of all our pilgrimages – to listen for the cock crowing every time we allow our own great expectations, in whatever field or sphere we may cherish them, to dominate our horizons and blot out the call to suffer, the call to lose our life, the call to take up the cross. We all have our reasons for wanting Jesus to be enthroned, our private ways of distorting his kingship so it suits our own aspirations or ambitions. The way to Jerusalem must always be also the way of thwarted expectations.

But, as every pilgrim knows, when you go to Jerusalem the primary reason remains that you go to meet God. Of course, we who read the New Testament know from Jesus himself, and from Paul, that those who worship the true

God are not bound by geography. Neither in Jerusalem nor in Samaria will they worship, for the Father seeks people to worship in spirit and in truth (John 4.20–4). That, however, is a radical Christian innovation, untrue to the thousand years that went before. 'Like as the hart desireth the water brooks, so longeth my soul after thee, O God; when shall I come to appear before the presence of God?' We should not be so quick to spiritualize those words from Psalm 42 as to miss the point they make in their context: this is a prayer that the psalmist may be allowed to return from exile, to return to Jerusalem, to come back, spatially, geographically, into the very presence of God.

And it is so even to this day, in bizarre ways. It is often said that Jerusalem is a focal point for three great religions, Judaism, Christianity and Islam; but it is actually a focal point for four, because to these we must add another 'ism', namely Tourism. Tourism is the modern, secular version of pilgrimage, in which we go to famous places, or to see well-known sights, not to meet God or to receive healing or blessing, but to see things that our culture tells us we ought to see, to expand our own horizons and experiences, to buy souvenirs to make us feel good when we're back home, to take photos and videos so that we can steal something of the reality of the place and make it part of our own private reality. You go to Jerusalem, or Athens, or Venice, or anywhere else, to worship the god of secularism, the god of a liberal culture that tells you to observe from a critical distance, but not to get involved. To sense the magic of the place, and then to buy postcards. To say a prayer perhaps, if that's your kind of thing, but not to stay on your knees all day. We've got to get on to the museum, or back to the hotel for tea. Our reality must remain undisturbed. Take no notice of that cock crowing in the background.

Because the way to Jerusalem stands for the way into the

presence of the living God, the one who is always disturbing, never tame, always hiding from the clever and the learned and always revealing himself to babies. Jerusalem is a place where it's very easy to be religious, and also very easy to use religion as a tree behind which, like naked Adam, to hide from the personal presence of the God who comes to ask questions: where are you? who are you? what are you doing? Jerusalem is a place where it's very easy to sense the presence of God, or at least the warm place in the bed where he once was, and also very easy to distort that sense so that God gets remade in your own image, to serve your own ends, to bolster your own ambitions or to underwrite your ideologies.

And the test of whether pilgrimage is genuine is therefore the question, whether you're prepared for God to remake you instead, lovingly to break the brittle 'you' that you've so carefully constructed, to soften the clay in his hands until it's ready to be remoulded, and then to make out of you what he had in mind all along, which may be quite different from what you wanted or expected. Jerusalem is a symbol of *God's* great expectations, which will by no means coincide with our own. The only true way to go on pilgrimage to Jerusalem is to go, like Abraham, not knowing where you are going, or who it is that you will meet when you get there; to suspend a clinging and anxious belief as well as a sceptical unbelief, and simply to *be*: to be open, to be still, to wait in silence for the strange God who still comes to those who wait in silence. The road to Jerusalem stands for the deeply inviting, yet deeply threatening, journey into the presence of the one true God, where all is known and all is unknown, where all is asked and all is promised. And that, whether or not we ever make the geographical journey to Jerusalem itself, is the pilgrimage to which we are all summoned.

Each of us is bidden and beckoned to come on pilgrimage to find the living God. Oh, it's easy enough to be a tourist of Christianity, to enjoy the music, to say a quick prayer, and then to shake ourselves free, to get out for a cup of coffee, before the hard questions get asked, before the demands are issued, before the cross looms up out of the mist. Every Christian, every Christian institution, every church, every cathedral, goes through cycles of discovering God, adoring God, institutionalizing God, domesticating God, denying God, and then, please God, rediscovering God again. The greatest Christian institutions are those that remember, like the sculptor deliberately leaving the work unfinished lest he be guilty of hubris, that God cannot be contained or imprisoned, and will always break out elsewhere and do things we didn't expect. The greatest Christian institutions keep, metaphorically speaking, a few cocks around to crow when we don't want them to, to remind us of the ever-present danger of remaking God in our own image. It is part of Christian pilgrimage to be reminded that we are dust, and to dust we shall return. And those who are truly learning the pilgrim way learn to listen, in scripture and sacrament, in silence and in suffering, for the voice of the one who loves them more deeply than they love themselves, and who therefore must ask us the questions we have not dared to face, and must ask of us that which we would rather not give.

Come, then, to God with your expectations great or small, muddled or over-eager. Come to the one who is the true object of all our desires and longings, and who must therefore firmly but gently challenge all lesser loves and hopes. Come, like Abraham, not knowing where you are going, but trusting the one who is leading you. Take up your cross, and come to where the bed is still warm with the presence of Jesus, to where the fresh bread and the sweet wine still speak of his own pilgrimage and passion, and add your voice, and your own language and accent, to the chorus that increases day by day. Come to the new Jerusalem, whose citizens you already are, to the place where God himself will dwell with his people, and will himself wipe away every tear from every eye. Come to the city where the cocks crow, no longer to accuse the disloyalties of the night, but to greet the new day, and the children of that day. That city, unknown and well known, is the goal of our pilgrimage; and our present prayer and present pain, our Lenten fast and earthly pilgrimages, are roads towards it and metaphors for it. We are going up to Jerusalem; and the Son of Man will come with his angels in the glory of his Father. All will be made clear, all will be healed, all will be forgiven.

SIX

The Way up the Mountain

IN THE MIDDLE of Galilee, four or five miles from Nazareth, there stands a mountain. It is circular, almost perfect in its symmetry, like the top half of a great round ball emerging from the Galilean plain. When you get to the top, where it flattens off, you can see the whole of central southern Galilee spread out around you. You look down on the dozens of little villages where Jesus walked and talked. Welcome to Mount Tabor, famous locally as the Mount of the Transfiguration.

Actually, we don't know for sure if that's where it happened. The Gospels place this incident one week after Caesarea Philippi, when Peter recognized Jesus as Messiah, and Jesus summoned the disciples to take up the cross and follow him to Jerusalem. Caesarea Philippi, as we saw in the previous chapter, stands at the extreme north of Galilee, on the slopes of Mount Hermon. Jesus may have stayed in that area, and then taken Peter, James and John up Mount Hermon, rather than coming south through Galilee to climb Mount Tabor. Hermon is higher, more remote, more inaccessible, which is no doubt why the long traditions of Christian pilgrimage have found it more convenient to celebrate the transfiguration on Tabor instead.

Nothing much hinges on it. What matters is what mountains mean in the story of God's people. Moses came to Mount Sinai, and saw the bush burning, and discovered himself to be in the personal, close and dangerous presence of God. That moment of commission led to the subsequent visit to Sinai, where he went up to wait upon God, to receive the law of God, to plead with God when Israel sinned. When he came down, the skin of his face was shining, because he had been with God. So too Elijah, at his moment of deepest desolation, made his way from Mount Carmel, where he had slaughtered the prophets of Baal, to Mount Sinai, where after the earthquake, wind and fire there came a still small voice, asking 'What are you doing here, Elijah?', and commissioning him afresh, assuring him that God's strange purposes were going ahead, despite appearances, and despite his depression. Abraham's strangest and darkest dealing with God took place on a mountain. David lifted his eyes to the hills, and saw them as a symbol of the presence of God.

I can still remember the moment, in my first year of theological study, when I realized for the first time the way in which Old Testament themes come rushing together in fresh configurations in the New Testament. It was a sudden moment of joy, comparable in its way with my first hearing of Mendelssohn's Violin Concerto a few years before, and with falling in love a year or two afterwards. And it was the story of the transfiguration that did it. Here, once again, Moses and Elijah meet God on the mountain. History is suddenly telescoped together; past and present are fused into one, yes, and future too, because the transfiguration points forward, as Luke says in his account, to Jesus' departure, his Exodus, which he was to accomplish at Jerusalem. And the voice from the cloud, the same voice that announced the Ten Commandments to Moses, and that whispered a gentle rebuke and recommissioning to Elijah, now speaks of Jesus and Jesus only: this is my son, my beloved one, in whom I am well pleased; listen to him. The next time anyone will suggest that Jesus is the son of God it will be Caiaphas, in the trial narrative, and then the centurion at the foot of the cross. The whole story of redemption comes together into one place. Just as from Mount Tabor you can look out over that whole sweep of Galilee, so from the Mount of Transfiguration you can survey the whole of God's redemptive history and see it as one.

But of course the strangest thing in the story is the actual transfiguration itself. Jesus was transformed, so that his face shone like the sun, and his clothes themselves became shining white. This is not, in itself, a revelation of Jesus' divinity. If that were so, we would have to conclude that Moses, too, was divine, because of his own transfiguration on Mount Sinai. The glory which shone from Jesus' face on the mountain is the glory of a human being, made in God's image, and now totally open to God, totally possessed by God, totally reflecting God, totally on fire with God. Seeing this human being, we are seeing God, God in a mirror, God through the looking-glass, God present as in the burning bush but now in the shining face, and even clothes, of a man amongst men:

> O World invisible, we view thee,
> O World intangible, we touch thee,
> O World unknowable, we know thee,
> Inapprehensible, we clutch thee!

And it is because of this that the path of Christian pilgrimage has always included the way up the mountain. Many religious traditions have sought the intimate presence of the unknowable God; the other two great monotheistic faiths, Judaism and Islam, have had their mystics who have returned from the journey into the unknown to speak of the one God in strangely familiar terms. But the Christian tradition has emphasized two great complementary truths about mountain-top experiences, times of special and transforming intimacy with God. On the one hand, they are for anyone and everyone, and if you're missing out on them you may want to review, and renew, your life of prayer and waiting upon God. On the other hand, the importance of such experiences lies not in the experiences themselves, but in what they do to us, what they prepare us for, what they commission us to.

Many Christians in the Western tradition are startled to be told that transfiguration is an experience that can happen to anyone. We have quietly assumed that such things are either for Jesus only, or, if we remember about Moses, for very special people only. There is, however, a tradition, submerged but still present in Western Christianity, but very much alive in the Eastern Orthodox churches, that discovers in a whole variety of ways the transforming presence of God, catching up human beings in a quite literal blaze of glory, informing both prayer and theology, witness and Christian living, enabling people to survive and even to celebrate as Christians in the midst of great hardship and persecution, enabling them also to see the reflection of God in a new way in other people, and in the whole order of creation. In that tradition, prayer is not a perfunctory duty, but a deep constant ingrained activity, invoking and enjoying the presence of God with every breath, every heartbeat, until some have even come to experience, and remarkably enough to share with those around a physical brightness, a radiance, for all the world like that of Jesus on the mountain. Listen to this account, by a nineteenth-century Russian journalist, Nicholas Motovilov, of his visit in 1831 to Father Seraphim of Sarov, a great holy man and elder of the Church, a *Staretz*:

Father Seraphim gripped me firmly by the shoulders and said: 'My friend, both of us, at this moment, are in the Holy Spirit, you and I. Why won't you look at me?'

'I can't look at you, Father, because the light flashing from your eyes and face is brighter than the sun and I'm dazzled!'

'Don't be afraid, friend of God, you yourself are shining just like I am; you too are now in the fullness of the grace of the Holy Spirit, otherwise you wouldn't be able to see me as you do.'

Then I looked at the Staretz, the holy man, and was panic-stricken. Picture, in the sun's orb, in the most dazzling brightness of its noon-day shining, the face of a man who is talking to you. You see his lips moving, the expression in his eyes, you hear his voice, you feel his arms round your shoulders, and yet you see neither his arms, nor his body, nor his face, you lose all sense of yourself, you can see only the blinding light which spreads everywhere, lighting up the layer of snow covering the glade, and igniting the flakes that are falling on us both like white powder.

'What do you feel?' asked Father Seraphim.

'An amazing well-being!' I replied ... 'I feel a great calm in my soul, a peace which no words can express ... A strange, unknown delight ... An amazing happiness ... I'm amazingly warm ... There's no scent in all the world like this one!'

'I know,' said Father Seraphim, smiling ... 'This is as it should be, for divine grace comes to live in our hearts, within us ... the kingdom of God is just the grace of the Holy Spirit, living in us, warming us, enlightening us, filling the air with his scent, delighting us with his fragrance and rejoicing our hearts with an ineffable gladness.'

That is perhaps the most dramatic example recorded in modern times, though there are constant hints elsewhere of strange things which in our rationalistic and sceptical age we pooh-pooh and discount. The transfiguration has come to stand, in Eastern theology at least, for the belief that the spiritual world is very near at hand, not far up in the sky, off in some metaphysical space beyond our normal reach; and for the belief that God's promise of salvation includes God's intention to transform us into his own likeness, a transformation that God longs to begin even here and now.

This openness to the unseen dimension, the realm of the angels, is a constant challenge. Where are the angels today? asks the poet Francis Thompson, and answers that

> The drift of pinions, would we hearken,
> Beats at our own clay-shuttered doors.

It is our blindness, our arrogant refusal to admit of any reality that won't go into a test-tube, that prevents us from opening ourselves to God's dimensions of reality, in the angelic world and elsewhere:

> The angels keep their ancient places;
> Turn but a stone, and start a wing!
> 'Tis ye, 'tis your estrangèd faces,
> That miss the many-splendoured thing.

The way up the mountain, then, stands for us today, first, as a reminder, a rebuke and an invitation. A reminder that there are levels and depths of spirituality that are open to all of us, but from which we hide ourselves, perhaps in our heart of hearts quite deliberately, from fear of what the transforming presence of the burning God might do if he were truly given free rein in our hearts and lives. A reminder, thus, of the fact that all of life is, so to speak, 'sacramental'; that the world is charged with the grandeur of God, and that what we do with water, bread and wine in the official sacraments of the Church is simply the tell-tale sign of reality in a world where God's glory will flame out unexpectedly. Thus, too, a rebuke: that we so often content ourselves with going through the motions of a pattern of Christian discipleship that stays on the surface, that doesn't get too excited or exciting, when not far away there are levels of reality, of God's reality, waiting to be discovered, if we will take time and care, if we will seek silence and grace, if we will invoke the Holy Spirit to transform us.

I suspect for many of us the time when we come closest to that reality is in worship, as (for instance) glorious music lifts hearts and imaginations, in tune with the meanings perhaps of a great building, a holy place, a wonderful fellowship, into the presence of God. But God's invitation is then that we should build on that; to make that the starting-point, not the finishing-point, of our own personal spiritual journey, the journey up the mountain, the journey into the presence of God. And if we're not making that journey, all our Lenten disciplines, all our to-ing and fro-ing of resolution and aspiration, of doubt and disappointment, of puzzlement and rededication, are in danger of becoming mere self-centred games. I do not know in what ways the living presence of God will transform your life today and tomorrow. But I do know that the way up the mountain is an inalienable part of our Christian pilgrimage, and that to remain in spiritual flatland is to condemn ourselves to spiritual boredom, which leads to doubt and even to spiritual death, denying that there are such things as mountains at all, just because we can't be bothered to climb them.

To change the image for a moment: many today, including alas many practising Christians, live in a perpetual spiritual winter. They regard photographs of buds and blossoms as fairytale fantasies, things that don't happen in the real world. And if our present lifestyles, both in church and in our everyday lives, don't allow space for mountain-climbing, for fresh springtimes of the spirit, we should take steps to put matters right. Deep, rich and transforming experiences of the presence of God are not reserved for special categories of people. They are on offer for everyone.

But, finally, the importance of spiritual mountain-top experiences lies not in themselves but in what God teaches us through them, and what God prepares us for, and commissions us for, through them. It is of the utmost significance that, in all three synoptic Gospels, the transfiguration occurs immediately after Jesus has set his face to go to Jerusalem and to suffer, and has challenged his disciples to take up the cross and follow him.

Spiritual experiences, great moments of illumination and transformation, are never given simply so that we may enjoy them for their own sake. We live in an experience-oriented culture, which teaches us to value experiences for themselves. The danger for the Christian, whether he or she be Catholic or Orthodox, Anglican or Baptist, evangelical, mystical, or charismatic, is to think that one's experiences of the presence and love of God are somehow a possession, given simply to be enjoyed, clung to, celebrated in themselves. That way danger lies, not least such as is referred to in the old jibe about mysticism of the wrong sort, that it begins in mist, centres upon I, and ends in schism.

But the abuse of God's gifts does not invalidate the real use. And, whether the gift be a mystical awareness of God's presence, a charismatic gift like tongues, an experience of transfiguration, a strong sense of God's presence in the liturgy of the Church, or whatever, the gift is given within a context of vocation and to strengthen us for that vocation.

And if the experience is truly an experience of the God we know in Jesus Christ, that vocation will always include the call to take up the cross; and the illumination may well take place at the very moment when the cross has been endured or embraced in some fresh way. The Russian church in the nineteenth century, knowing great experiences of the transforming presence of God, was being prepared, I believe, for the great trials and persecutions that were to come in the present century. In the poem I've already quoted, Francis Thompson, who knew more than most about melancholy and desolation, writes of the sudden transforming presence of angels, and of Jesus himself, in the midst of a London where he was in deepest despair:

> But (when so sad thou canst not sadder)
> Cry; – and upon thy so sore loss
> Shall shine the traffic of Jacob's ladder
> Pitched betwixt Heaven and Charing Cross.
>
> Yea, in the night, my Soul, my daughter,
> Cry, – clinging Heaven by the hems;
> And lo, Christ walking on the water,
> Not of Genesareth, but Thames!

A deeply genuine Christian spirituality, then, is not about wallowing self-indulgently in joyful feelings of the presence of God, though God knows most of us could use more times of stillness and enjoyment of God's loving presence than we normally make space for. It is rooted in the pain of the world, often in our own pain and distress, and calls us to minister to the pain of the world, to bring God's love into that pain, and often to feel more of it ourselves as we do so. If your vocation, your God-given path, should lead you in the way of pain, your own or someone else's, that may itself be a sign that you are called to make another journey up the mountain, to glimpse the vision of glory once more and to gather fresh strength for the journey. The first thing Jesus had to do on coming down the mountain was to heal a demon-possessed boy. The final thing he had to do was to go to Jerusalem and die. But he did the one and the other strengthened and encouraged by what had happened on the mountain. From the top of the mountain you can see the villages and lanes of the way ahead laid out before you. When you go down to the valley, you need to remember what you saw on the mountain, if you are not to lose your way.

Take time out from your busy travelling, then, come up the mountain, and wait patiently for God. Perhaps it's time at last to do what you've always promised yourself and never got round to: to set aside time for prayer and meditation on Scripture; to go on retreat; to reorder the habits of life in which you've got stuck, so as to make fresh room for the God who waits to show you his glory. Perhaps it's time to seek out a spiritual director who may gently help you to move forward on the twisty road up the mountain. Perhaps it's time to expose yourself again to the possibility that you too might hear a voice, might glimpse glory, might fall on your face in terror and awe, might be grasped afresh by the majesty of Jesus.

And to those who do climb the mountain comes the promise, echoing the transfiguration story but pointing beyond it, from the letter of John: 'Beloved, we are God's children now, and it does not yet appear what we shall be; but we know that when Jesus appears, we shall be like him, for we shall see him as he is (1 John 3.2–3). The road up the mountain is not for the casual tourist or the faint-hearted. But the view from the top is out of this world.

SEVEN

The Way to Gethsemane

WHY DID JESUS stay in Gethsemane?

It wasn't his normal stopping-place. Usually, after a day in Jerusalem, he took the twelve back to their lodging in Bethany, just over the brow of the Mount of Olives. That little journey involved leaving the city on its steep eastern side, going right down into the deep Kidron valley, and then just as sharply up again, higher than before, up and over the Mount of Olives, to Bethany the other side. On that short but steep journey, they would pass Gethsemane just after crossing the brook Kidron, at the lowest point of the trip. The word 'Gethsemane' itself derives from the Hebrew and Aramaic word for an olive-press; doubtless the original garden was an olive orchard, containing some of the thousands of olive trees that cluster on the slope of the hill. As with most holy sites around Jerusalem, there is dispute today as to its exact first-century location, but it must have been more or less at the foot of the Mount of Olives. Why, on the last occasion, did Jesus stop there?

Consider the two more obvious options open to Jesus that night. His actions and words during the previous days had spoken of the coming kingdom of God as something which was about to break in, challenging the rule of darkness with the dawn of the new day. His demonstration in the Temple had indicated that the present system was under God's judgement; his last meal had indicated that the new

81

Exodus, the moment of liberation, was now at last at hand. He had declared at the supper table that he would not drink again of the fruit of the vine until he drank it new in the kingdom of God. His followers, eager for hints and signs, and all too ready to interpret them in terms of the agendas they had cherished all along, were ready to move at his order. They had plenty of friends and supporters in the city, who would no doubt be ready to swing a sword for Jesus and the kingdom. A surprise night attack, with or without the twelve legions of angels, but with Jesus and his remarkable power and authority leading the way, and by morning the kingdom of God, in the sense they longed for, would have come. Jesus would be the new king, and they would sit at his right hand and his left in his kingdom. That was the first option, and for Jesus' followers doubtless the most obvious one.

So why, after their liberation banquet, did Jesus not give the command to move back up into the city, to do what they knew they had come for? Why did he stay in Gethsemane?

Or take the other option. Supposing Jesus had decided against the political, military route. Supposing he had decided that the kingdom of God was after all a matter of private piety, of inner spiritual disposition, of devotion and prayer: a spirituality to be cultivated, not an action to be undertaken? Supposing he had thought that God's promise of eventual justice and peace belonged to a different world altogether, and that his task, having announced this hope, was to wait for God to do it in his own way and time? Having made his point, he could then have quietly withdrawn to the countryside, to the desert, to wait and pray. He could have led the twelve over the Mount of Olives, to Bethany certainly, or further, down the far side, all the way down to the Jordan valley. Like King David fleeing from Absalom, they could have been across the Jordan by morning, well away from betrayers or temple guards. They could have established a community there, said the Lord's Prayer three times a day, and waited for God to do whatever God was going to do. They might have looked remarkably like the sect who lived at Qumran.

So why did Jesus not take this route? Why did he stay in Gethsemane? We are bound to face this question, whether we go on an actual pilgrimage to the Holy Land or stay at home and make the pilgrimage in heart and mind through the events of Jesus' passion. The Church has not found it easy to stay in Gethsemane with Jesus, perhaps because it has regularly preferred one of the other options: either to get on with the business of establishing a worldly kingdom of God, or to retreat, to withdraw, into the cultivation of a private piety and a quietist hope. But for the Christian who wants to follow Jesus himself on the pilgrim way, the question cannot be avoided. Why did Jesus stay in Gethsemane? And what does it mean for us to stay there with him?

To find the answer we must go back to that strange saying about the cup, which darkly foreshadows the scene in the garden. 'Can you drink the cup,' said Jesus to James and John, 'the cup that I drink? Can you be baptized with the baptism I am baptized with?' (Mark 10.38). They wanted to share his kingly power, to sit on either side of him when he was enthroned in Jerusalem. It's pretty clear what sort of a kingdom they thought he was going to establish; and it's pretty clear that Jesus was trying to tell them, to warn them, that things weren't going to be like that, that the kingdom wouldn't be like that, that God wasn't like that. The kingdom would come, but it would come through the drinking of a cup, through a baptism, through something Jesus had to do, had to undergo, which they could not yet take in.

And then, in the garden, Jesus faced the choice himself,

and shrank from it. 'Abba, Father! All things are possible to you; take this cup away from me; yet, not what I want, but what you want' (Mark 14.36). If there was another way, Jesus would grasp it eagerly. Everything inside him recoiled from the cup that was held out to him. This is no heroic scene, with a brave martyr going fearlessly to his death. But then this was no ordinary martyrdom. This was the real battle, with the real enemy. This was the time of trial, which he had urged his followers to pray that they be spared. This was the moment when the forces of darkness were about to unleash their power, the time of great suffering through which God's kingdom-plan had to pass if it were to reach its goal. And to face this moment, Jesus went to the place where King David had passed as he retreated in mourning from the rebellion of Absalom, with half his household betraying him. This was the place where the kingdom was to be battled over in tears and in the face of disloyalty.

It was not just human adversaries Jesus was facing – soldiers, guards, even one of his own friends turned traitor. It was the concentration of all those unseen forces, that opposed the kingdom of God because they knew it to be the powerful opponent of their own kingdom-dreams: the forces of oppression and violence, the unseen pull that makes people fight rather than be reconciled, that makes them choose brutality rather than humanity, tribe rather than world, self rather than God. These forces had opposed Jesus throughout his public career, sometimes shrieking at him from the lips of some poor deranged spirit, sometimes carping at him in the sneers of the religious, sometimes issuing threats against him from the royal palace. Now they gathered together in the hour of darkness, and Jesus knew he had to go and meet them, naked, alone. His followers, though, must not be sucked into the vortex of evil. They must 'watch and pray, that they may not come into the time of trial' (Mark 14.38). This is a task that Jesus must do all by himself; and the anticipation of it causes him agony, so that he begins to sweat great drops, like blood. Why did he stay there? And what does it mean for us to stay there with him?

Part of the answer is found in another cup. Gethsemane is partly interpreted in terms of what immediately preceded it. That evening, at the supper table, Jesus took the cup of wine, and declared: 'This is my blood of the new covenant, shed for you and for many for the forgiveness of sins' (Matthew 26.28). This was a Passover meal with a radical difference. The great Jewish festivals looked simultaneously backwards to what God had done in the past, and forwards to what he would do in the future. Passover, specifically, looked back to the time when God liberated his people from slavery in Egypt, when God had established his covenant with Israel at Sinai; and it therefore looked forward to the time when God would establish his new covenant with her, the new covenant promised in Jeremiah, in which she would be set free not merely from political slavery but from the deeper and darker slavery to the power of sin and evil. 'The days are coming when I will make a new covenant with Israel and Judah, not like the covenant I made when I brought them out of Egypt. I will be their God, and they shall be my people . . . for I will forgive their wrongdoing and remember their sin no more' (Jeremiah 31.31–4).

At the supper table Jesus was saying that the moment had come. It would be established through his own suffering and death. The cup of the new covenant was given to Jesus' followers because of the cup that Jesus himself would drink, even though contemplating it in the garden broke him apart. Jesus had to stay in Gethsemane because he had chosen the different way, the true kingdom-way, the way of obedient suffering through which God would establish the new covenant. The way to Gethsemane is therefore through and from the upper room.

We don't know exactly where Jesus celebrated the Last Supper with his followers. (Ingenious guides, ancient and modern, have not hesitated to propose various locations. Strong and early legends place it in the house of St Mark, in the south-west part of the old city, where today there is a Syrian Orthodox church of St Mark. This is less than a mile on foot from Gethsemane.) But the significance of the Last Supper is of course far more important than the location. This was the meal in which Jesus drew together the strands of his whole ministry, his whole project. This was where all the roads led, from the Jordan, from Galilee, from the mountain-top, and from within Jerusalem itself. This was the action which said: here is the kingdom of God, and you who share this meal with me share in that kingdom. This was the action which interpreted Jesus' approaching death in terms of God's age-old purposes for Israel: the plan that, through Israel's new covenant, her God, the creator, would bring about his new world of justice, peace and forgiveness.

This, equally importantly, was the action that interpreted those longed-for purposes of God in terms of Jesus himself and his imminent death. It was a moment of vision, of glory, of rich mystery and celebration, a moment to rival the mountain-top. Those of us who return in heart and mind to the upper room day after day, week after week, to do again what Jesus did there, are invited to share in this mystery, this celebration, which constitutes us again and again as Jesus' people, the people of the new covenant, the people called into being by his death and resurrection, the people formed and shaped by the word 'forgiveness'. We can argue about doctrine, we can worry about ethics, we can get into difficulties over ritual and words and rules and regulations.

But when we take the bread and the cup, and do with them what Jesus did, we are his people, for better or for worse, claiming his life and death as the source of our own life and the hope in our own death.

And we are therefore the people called in our turn to go and wait in Gethsemane. We are the people called now to wrestle with the strange purposes of God in the time between the passion of Jesus and the final redemption of the whole of creation. We are the people called neither to take up arms and force the kingdom upon an unwilling world nor to run away into a private spirituality. We who drink his cup in the eucharist are the people called, as James and John would be called, to drink the cup which he drank, to undergo the baptism which he underwent. We are the people called into Passiontide, into Gethsemane-tide, into prayer and fasting, into betrayal and suffering, into the ambiguous and agonizing position of wrestling with the purposes of God, into knowing that we might have got it wrong, into wondering in anguish if maybe there's a different way after all, into being misunderstood by friends and family, into fightings without and fears within. The disciples fell asleep in the garden; we are called to stay awake, to be alert, to see what the issues are and what stand must be taken, to do business with the one Jesus called Abba, Father, even if voices all around us, and even within us, tell us we might be getting it all horribly wrong.

This calling becomes focused on three things in particular.

To begin with, we are called to be the people of the new covenant; and that means, to be the people who live by God's gift and call of forgiveness. This remains as hard a way as ever. In many societies today, including alas some so-called Christian ones, forgiveness is not even valued, let alone attempted or accomplished. Ultimately, it is only possible when we have the cross before our eyes, and when we are fed in mind and heart, as well as body, from the broken bread and poured out wine of the Lord's table. But forgiveness remains the ground on which, as Christians, we claim to stand; and we are called to model it day by day and week by week, precisely in the relationships which cause us pain and about which we'd rather be able to go on grumbling. This is so in interpersonal relationships, within a congregation, among colleagues and friends and neighbours; and it is so in what you might call inter-tribal relationships, whether it be between classes or cultures, not least in the crowded little island called Great Britain, or between actual tribes and races, in the Middle East, or the Balkans, or Northern Ireland. And to stand on that ground, rather than go forward into attack mode or backwards into retreat, avoiding the problem rather than dealing with it, we need to wrestle in prayer, in our own private Gethsemanes, until the way opens up before us.

Second, as Jesus makes clear, we are called to live by a different model of leadership. The recognized rulers lord it over their subjects, and their great ones make them feel the weight of their authority. But it mustn't be like that with you. We are called to struggle for, to bear witness to, a way of leadership which is neither the bullying arrogance of the tyrant nor the weak vacillation of the populist. In the Church itself, and in leadership roles within society, we must struggle for the third way, the way of the suffering servant, sharing and bearing the pain of his people.

The Church has usually been as bad at this as the rest of the world. But Gethsemane remains as a summons to prayer and witness and readiness to follow God's vocation wherever it may lead. It stands for the vocation of the Church in the midst of a world that longs for the kingdom of God but doesn't call it that, that struggles for justice and peace but succeeds only in creating more wars and tribal divisions, a

world in which forgiveness is for weaklings and suffering is
the opposite of success. The Church is attacked today by
voices which want us to take up the sword and lead a charge
on wickedness, and by other voices which want us to retire
quietly into the role of spirituality, leaving Caesar to look
after Caesar's kingdom while we cultivate the inner kingdom of the soul. The Church is routinely betrayed by those
from within its own ranks who side with the enemy, who
come as friends but whose kiss is deadly. But our calling
remains the way to Gethsemane: to struggle in prayer on
behalf of the kingdom of God at the place where the world
is still in great pain, and to be ready for our own vocation,
whether or not it is the one we would have chosen ourselves.
In particular, we are called to model a different style of
leadership.

Third, we all face individual moments of struggle with
vocation: the vocation of the young, seeking the way forward
for a lifetime of active service; the vocation of the middle-aged,
working through the twists and turns, the new opportuni-
ties and disappointments, of mid-life; the senior vocations,
to model and live out the way of the cross in the face of
increasing weakness and approaching death, both one's
own and that of those one loves. If we cannot reflect on
these things in Gethsemane of all places, then we have
indeed forgotten what we are about.

To all of us, in these moments, the message of Gethsemane is loud and clear: do not imagine that because you
find yourself in turmoil, struggling with turbulent fear and
uncertainty, this means you have come the wrong way or
arrived at the wrong place. The idea that Christians should
always have nothing but inner peace and tranquillity is at
best a half-truth, at worst a romantic or existentialist betrayal
of the Jesus of Gethsemane. This is the way our Master
trod, and he has invited us to follow him, to watch with

him, to wait and pray with him. If we have shared his bread and his cup, shall we not also share his agony in the garden? If we have heard his call to discipleship, shall we at this moment of all moments run away and flee, or perhaps even join in with his betrayers and accusers?

Equally, if we have something difficult to face, whether it be the need to forgive someone, the call to a style of action and leadership which goes against the grain of the world, the chance to do something difficult but important at work or elsewhere, or the call to face suffering and death, Gethsemane is the place which reminds us that the real battle must be won on our knees in advance. Jesus knew deep within himself that he had to face Caiaphas and Pilate, temple guards and Roman soldiers, weeping women and mocking crowds, betrayal, torture and death. He went from the moment of ecstasy and revelation in the upper room to the moment of agony in the garden of Gethsemane, in order to wrestle in prayer with his Father over what was still to come. If he needed to do that, how much more do we. Let us, in our pilgrimages, make space in our schedules and our hearts to stay awake, and watch in the garden with our Lord, that when morning comes we may be strong to do his will.

EIGHT

The Way of the Cross

THE OLD CITY of Jerusalem is built on a hill with steep
sides. It is itself bisected by the Tyropoean valley, which
runs more or less north to south. Many of the city streets
slope steeply; those that run from east to west go down
sharply before they rise up again the other side. Every Good
Friday, a huge throng of pilgrims from all over the world
crowds in to one of those east–west streets.

Like most streets in the Old City, it is seldom as much as
twenty feet wide, often more like ten. Packed together along
it are shops and cafés and street vendors. There are the
sights and sounds of cooking, bargaining, arguing. Children
are playing under everybody's feet.

This particular street begins on the north side of the
old Temple mount, close to where the Roman fortress once
stood, overlooking the Temple in case of riots during festivals. It goes down into the middle of what is now still, just
about, the Muslim quarter, the scene of much recent
anguish as settlers from the right-wing Jewish community
do their best to buy up property and change the city's
demographic balance. Then, near the lowest point, the
street turns sharply to the left along the line of the valley,
then sharply right again, rising up steeply towards the west
side of the city. Two more jogs left and right would, in
Jesus' day, bring you through the old city wall (though today
the wall is considerably further west), and to a small hill

outside. We have just walked the Via Dolorosa, the way of the cross.

Of course, historians and archaeologists disagree over which precise route that awful procession would have taken, early in the morning of the first Good Friday. It may be that Pilate tried Jesus at the citadel on the west side of the city, rather than in the fortress on the east, in which case the route would have been shorter and quite different. But from early days of Christian pilgrimage to Jerusalem, travellers have focused their attention on what is today the Via Dolorosa, marked out now with the various traditional 'stations of the cross', nine of them on the way to Golgotha and the remaining five within the Church of the Holy Sepulchre itself. In today's Jerusalem nothing much is free from commercialization, and you will see the 'Station Three Café', the 'Station Five Souvenir Shop', and be offered endless postcards and T-shirts displaying the street and its features. Pilgrims and tourists, pickpockets and touts, soldiers and beggars, jostle in the narrow streets and alleyways. We have no reason to suppose it was any different in Jesus' day.

On that day, that first Good Friday, there was a particular set of soldiers with a particular task to perform, which they did with their usual ruthless efficiency. It is all too easy to imagine the sense of horror and shock as the procession made its way along the narrow street, with the women raising their traditional ritual wailing, their grief compounded with the feeling of frustrated helplessness before their brutal political masters. (That feeling, too, is not entirely absent from Jerusalem today.) Here was a man on whom the hopes of many had rested, a man who had caught the imagination of the crowds, a man some of them had loved fiercely, on whose words they had hung, whose coming kingdom they had whispered of in dark alleyways and prayed for as they lit their evening candles. And out of sight, but certainly not out of mind, were eleven men stunned, in despair, who the previous night had had their feet washed by this condemned man; who had heard him say, 'A new commandment I give you: love one another, as I have loved you; no-one has greater love than this, than that a man lay down his life for his friends.'

It is that friendship that I want to reflect on now as we contemplate the way of the cross. The eleven didn't follow Jesus that day; one of them, according to John, did end up at the foot of the cross, perhaps because he, the disciple whom Jesus loved, was too young to be considered by the authorities worth arresting as he stood among the weeping women. The others did not follow Jesus on his last journey. They stayed behind locked doors, in shame and horror and grief and sheer disbelief at the way their golden dream had turned into a nightmare. Meanwhile, staggering through the city that April morning was the one who had called them his friends, who had shocked them by his actions at supper, who had spoken of the greatest thing that love could do, and who was now in the process of doing it.

Part of the point of the way of the cross is that, in the first instance, Jesus walks it alone. He does for his friends what they cannot do for themselves. It is a major problem in Christian devotion that when we think of the way of the cross we so often think of Jesus as the great example, with ourselves as simply imitating him. We follow the route of the stations of the cross, literally or metaphorically; we speak of taking up our cross and following Jesus; the great Bach Passions, in the chorales which express our response to the events of the passion, often lapse into the language of imitation, as though the point of Jesus' suffering and death were simply to show us the way to suffer and to die ourselves. But, though there is truth in that, the most important truth about the cross is that Jesus suffers so that others need not; that Jesus dies so that others may not. You do not speak of laying down your life for your friends if your friends are going to lay theirs down the next minute as well. When Jesus washed his friends' feet, they did not respond by washing his.

What Jesus did on the cross is not, therefore, simply an example, even the supreme example, of some general truth either about how people should behave or about what God is like. The cross only becomes an example, as and when it does, because it is first an achievement, an accomplishment. We can only truly speak of following Jesus on the way of the cross if we have first stood back and watched in awe and gratitude as he walks it alone on our behalf.

You see, the achievement of the cross is presented throughout the New Testament as the pinnacle of the plan whereby the creator God, the God of Israel, had purposed to save his world. This implies, of course, that the world is not simply perplexed, needing good advice; nor simply misguided, needing good leadership; nor simply muddled, needing good examples. The world, in the early Christian (and Jewish) analysis, is sick and needs to be healed; it is sinful and needs to be forgiven; it is under alien lordship, and yearns for the kingdom of God. Jesus walks the way of the cross as the healer of the world's ills, the lamb whose death brings forgiveness, the king coming in his strange kingdom. 'Jesus of Nazareth', said Pilate's sign, 'the King of the Jews'; even Pilate, who didn't know what truth was, knew what Jesus was. 'What I have written, I have written.'

Jesus is in truth the King of the Jews, the climax of the saving purpose of God. That purpose, planned long before in the story of Israel, God's servant-people, matured through the years of suffering and exile, was now concentrated on the city at the centre of the world, the people at the centre of God's plan, and the man at the centre of God's people.

When Jesus walked the way of the cross, he was going to do what no-one else could do, or would ever need to do again. He was going to do battle with the forces of evil, and emerge victorious. He was going to bear our pains and carry our sorrows; to be wounded for our transgressions and bruised for our iniquities; to defeat death itself by his death. We cannot do that. Even to try would be a blasphemous nonsense, implying that what Jesus had done was ineffectual. His death was not a mere example of a general truth or style of action. It was unique.

Unless we recognize this singular and unrepeatable element in Jesus' way of the cross, Christianity collapses into just another way of being vaguely religious. If Jesus' death is only an example, not an achievement, there is no good news, only good advice; and the last two thousand years might suggest that the advice was not that good after all. If all we have in the story of Jesus is a fine example, it actually becomes quite depressing, since we discover how hard it is to follow that example, and how few even make the effort. But Christianity is not about making a bit more of a moral effort. It is about God finding us helpless and needy and coming to our rescue:

> Great God, in Christ you call our name,
> and then receive us as your own,
> not through some merit, right or claim,
> but by your gracious love alone.
> We strain to glimpse your mercy-seat
> and find you kneeling at our feet.

The way of the cross is therefore focused, first and foremost, on the unique and unrepeatable death of Jesus as the focal point of world history, the place where the pain and shame of the whole world was gathered into one place, inflicted on one person, one lonely individual stumbling through the steep streets of Jerusalem and out to an ugly little hill beyond. It made no sense to most people in the ancient world, as St Paul drily noted, and it makes no sense to most people today; but if this is not true – if it is not true that in Jesus of Nazareth the one true and living God came and lived in our midst and died on our behalf – then churches, basilicas and cathedrals are meaningless piles of stones, Christian liturgy is meaningless mumbo-jumbo, and beautiful church music is simply a fancy way of whistling in the dark. But if it is true – if it is true that the sickness of all the world was healed on Calvary, that the sin of all the world was forgiven on Calvary, that the alien rulers who have kept the world in chains were defeated on Calvary – then we cannot simply take Good Friday in our stride, as another little quirk in our interesting Christian calendar, but must stand still and silent, in hushed wonder, at the drama that is here played out, the drama that makes even Shakespeare look cheap and shallow, the play beside which the rest of our life is child's play. The story of Good Friday is either the most important thing in the world or it is a scandalous nonsense. There is no middle way.

We cannot help but tell this Good Friday story. We who live in the modern Western world, a world that is eager to forget the truth of Good Friday, eager to keep shops open, to go about ordinary business, to wipe away from the collective unconscious any sense that there might be healing and hope to be had in this awful and horrific story – we come back on Good Friday, and in heart and mind day by day and week by week, to tell that story again, to stop and stare in silence, because we have come to believe that there is no hope anywhere else. If this is not good news, there is no good news. If Jesus' way of the cross is not the way, the truth and the life, then we are all still looking for it, and should either eat, drink and be merry for tomorrow we die, or regard life as a sick joke and hand back our ticket.

This unique importance of Good Friday was movingly captured by John Carden, a missionary in Pakistan. In that Muslim culture he wrote words which resonate quite strongly with Jerusalem today, and which we could also easily translate into our own secular setting:

This morning I have had my annual, quite expected and yet still completely overwhelming dose of culture shock. And so great has been the strain today of seeing everybody going about their ordinary everyday working affairs as if nothing has happened, that it is only with the greatest difficulty that I have smothered my impulse to say to everybody I meet: '*But today is Good Friday*'.

I wanted to say it to the local *maulvi* ranting away in his Friday sermon, amplified, and penetrating into our every room;

I wanted to say it to the cinema crowd turning up in high-spirited herds to see *Sin* and *My heart beats for you* at our local cinema;

I wanted to say it to the hungry group taking a snack of generously peppered vegetables and fruit off saucers from a stall outside our cathedral gate;

I wanted to say it to the policeman boxing the ears of some offending cyclist;

I wanted to say it to the slim girl in the black veil, deep black eyes peering modestly on a naughty world;

I wanted to say it to the man rummaging around on the rubbish tip;

I wanted to say it to the youths riding three on a cycle from college;

I wanted them all to know the story which could alter the story of their lives.

To the man rummaging among the rubbish I wanted to say, 'Today shalt thou be with me in paradise'. To the girl in the black veil I wanted to tell the story of the women at the Cross. To the young men I wanted to repeat, 'Come, follow me'. To the hungry crowd, 'My flesh is meat indeed ...'. To the policeman, 'This man was truly the son of God.'

And if not the story, then the reality. I wanted to insert the reality of the Cross into the tissues of this life which goes on unhindered around.

Something good has happened today, something that cannot be confined to that little group of Christians who have taken off three hours to perform their religious observances. Something good has happened today which cannot be confined to churches and Christians, but must be out and about.

The goodness of forgiveness of sins;

the goodness of God's identification with men and women in their weakness and suffering;

the goodness of the one perfect and sufficient sacrifice, oblation and satisfaction for the sins of the whole world;

the goodness of God's act of reconciliation in Christ.

But today is Good Friday. Our task, as worshippers and would-be worshippers on the way of the cross, is, in John Carden's memorable phrase, 'to insert the reality of the Cross into the tissues of this life which goes on unhindered around'. How do we do that? What happens when we try? What does it then mean, having stood by silently and watched Jesus' unique pilgrimage on the Via Dolorosa, to take our courage in both hands and begin to follow him ourselves?

It means, to begin with, that we are Jesus' *friends*. 'No greater love than this; to lay down one's life for one's friends; and you are my friends . . .' We are not Jesus' acquaintances; we are not his slaves; we are not mere spectators in his life story. We are his friends, and Good Friday proves it. 'This is my friend, in whose sweet praise I all my days would gladly spend.'

How can you insert that into the tissues of your life? What does it mean when you get up in the morning and look in the mirror at one of Jesus' friends? Many of us, I fear, find it too extraordinary, perhaps too scary, to contemplate. Life goes on unhindered, and we keep Good Friday in a cupboard somewhere, to be brought out briefly with the hot cross buns and then hidden away again lest it disturb our normality. But to walk the way of the cross is not to perform some worrying religious ritual, laid upon us by a distant malevolent God who wants us to suffer and keeps himself detached from us while we do. It is to follow our friend where he has gone. It is to go out into each day, and to fall asleep each night, knowing that we are Jesus' friends; to undertake each task, to meet each person, to write each report, to teach each class, to tend each patient, knowing that as we do so we are defined as Jesus' friends. That is who we are. We are not Jesus' fans; we are his friends.

Second, it means that we are Jesus' *forgiven* friends. 'It is finished,' he said on the cross as he died (John 19.30). What was 'finished'? The work which the Father had given him to do. 'Having loved his own who were in the world, he loved them to the end,' to the uttermost (John 13.1). He did for them, uniquely, what only the love of God incarnate can do. He paid the price, he dealt with the weight of evil, he defeated the dark enemy that held us captive.

And yet many of us, much of the time, seem to prefer the darkness, the prison, to the sudden light of the new day. Many people, including many Christians, live out their lives under a weight of unforgiveness, blaming themselves for things that have gone wrong in their lives, blaming other people, particularly parents, children and spouses, for things that have gone wrong, feeling the weight of everyone else doing the same thing to them. Many people live with a sense of great obligation: obligation to God, to be impossibly perfect; obligation to other people, to be everything they need all the time; obligation to themselves, to achieve the highest results and position they possibly can. And since these obligations are usually impossible to attain, we live out our lives under a burden of guilt. Often people whom others regard as happy and sunny, outgoing and successful, are crippled inside with a sense of failure and inadequacy. And then there are, of course, the real sins, the real shortcomings: the violent temper, the sexual wrongdoings, the subtle cheating and lying and financial trickery to which most are tempted and many are prone.

And over all this sorry mess, guilt both real and imaginary, is written the words, 'It is finished.' Jesus has dealt with it. The only reason for hanging on to that guilt and sense of failure is if you want to stop being one of Jesus' friends. If you are a friend, you are a forgiven friend. Calvary achieved it. When you are invited to walk the way of the cross you are invited to do so as a forgiven friend. You've got nothing to prove any more. The only person worth trying to please loves you already so much that he died for you. If you are one of Jesus' friends, every breath you take you should breathe in that sense of relief, of letting the past go, of forgiveness. That is the birthright of all who travel the way of the cross. This is the reality to be inserted into the tissue of the rest of our life.

But, third, it means that we are Jesus' *suffering* friends. Everything in our success-driven culture rebels against this. We want to do well, to stay fit and healthy, to have a fulfilled and fulfilling life in which all our deepest dreams come true. We are in love with this world, and we expect as a matter of human rights that the world will reward our devotion. Many Christians today find it all too easy to translate the gospel into a message which fits with this seductive theme: turn to Jesus, and you won't have any problems, you'll be rich and healthy, and bad things won't happen to you. And then we are upset when it doesn't work out like that; when tragedy or illness strike, when we face daily difficulties and frustrations and pain and grief and loss. And because we have forgotten that on Good Friday Jesus made us his friends, his forgiven friends, we turn this too into a cause for gloom and guilt.

But the vocation to walk the way of the cross is the vocation to become Jesus' suffering friends. This, as the New Testament repeatedly reminds us, is a key part of the way in which the victory of the cross is to be implemented in all the world, as Jesus' friends walk behind him along their own Via Dolorosa, not just in Jerusalem but in every place where the world is in pain, in the hospice and the prison, in the slum and the job-centre, in the market-place and the kindergarten. These are often places of pain, and some of that pain will stick to us. Some of the suffering of the world will become our own. It is, after all, the wounded who are the real healers:

> The wounded surgeon plies the steel
> That questions the distempered part;
> Beneath the bleeding hands we feel
> The sharp compassion of the healer's art
> Resolving the enigma of the fever-chart.

And if that is true of Jesus, it is also true of those who go in his name to bring the news of his love to the places where the world is still in pain. To follow in the way of the cross

means to become Jesus' suffering friends, sustained only by
his suffering love:

> The dripping blood our only drink,
> The bloody flesh our only food:
> In spite of which we like to think
> That we are sound, substantial flesh and blood –
> Again, in spite of that, we call this Friday good.

And we are bound to reflect, in particular, that for millions
of Christians in today's world there is no choice about the
way of the cross. Two hundred million Christians worldwide
live in daily fear of secret police, vigilantes or state repression
and discrimination. In more than sixty countries worldwide,
Christians are harassed, abused, arrested, tortured or exe-
cuted specifically because of their faith. In the Sudan
Christians are enslaved and sometimes crucified. In Iran
they are assassinated. In Cuba they are imprisoned. In
China they are beaten to death. These are not wild rumours.
They are documented in detail, and they are continuing to
this day. For many of our brothers and sisters around the
world, Good Friday is every Friday, and every Monday,
Tuesday, Wednesday, Thursday, Saturday and Sunday as well.
Instead of a month of Sundays, imagine a year of Fridays.

And if our own suffering is of a more local, personal and
often invisible kind, we should remind ourselves, today of
all days, that we belong to a suffering family; that this is not
an unfortunate accident, a glitch in the system which our
own folly or sin has brought upon us, but that we are called
to be Jesus' suffering friends, people in whose own lives the
message of God's suffering yet all-conquering love resonates
out into the painful world around. How does a Christian
cope with suffering? Not by blaming him or herself; that
is to forget that we are Jesus' forgiven friends. Rather, by

trusting that the one who has called us friends is leading us along the same path that he walked, and is close by to give us strength and comfort in our time of need. This is the reality to be inserted into the tissues of this life which goes on unhindered all around.

Finally, therefore, because of Good Friday we are Jesus' *commissioned* friends. We are the ones through whom the unique victory of Calvary is to be put into practice in all the world. The call to follow Jesus, the call to take up the cross and walk behind him along the Via Dolorosa, is a call to be part of his kingdom-work, in and through which evil is to be defeated until the day when the Lamb who was slain is visibly enthroned as King of Kings and Lord of Lords. Precisely because of the nature of Jesus' victory on Calvary, it cannot be effective as a divine *fiat* from above, obliterating all opposition at a stroke. That would be to deny the very love which won the victory in the first place. Because Jesus' Good Friday victory was the victory of suffering love, it must be implemented gradually, as those who are themselves called in turn to embody that suffering love go out into the world to bring healing and hope to those who so badly need it. Every Christian, everyone who hears the call of Jesus to be his friend, is commissioned, precisely as a friend, to go and live the news of what our friend has done. Because we are forgiven friends, our commission can never result in our imagining that we are accomplishing something on our own, that our unaided efforts can bring in the kingdom. Because we are suffering friends, we can never use methods other than those of suffering love, the method of Jesus himself, to put our commission into effect. This is the reality to be inserted into the tissue of the rest of life.

'I have called you friends': forgiven friends, suffering friends, commissioned friends. Out of friendship to him, we watch in silence and reverence as he suffers and dies, alone, unique, accomplishing the world's salvation. Then, with awe and trembling, we find ourselves called to get up and follow on the way of the cross, to embody his love so that the world may be redeemed:

> Then take the towel, and break the bread,
> and humble us, and call us friends.
> Suffer and serve till all are fed,
> and show how grandly love intends
>> to work till all creation sings,
>> to fill all worlds, to crown all things.

NINE

The Way from the Tomb

THROUGHOUT THIS BOOK we have been travelling in heart and mind along the pilgrim way, reaching Jerusalem three chapters ago and, finally, Calvary. Now we arrive at our final destination.

But this is different. We are now to discover that, having arrived at the goal, the very idea of pilgrimage has been turned inside out; because with Easter Day the whole world is turned inside out, we ourselves are turned inside out, and God himself is turned inside out. Our final destination is not the empty tomb itself, central though that is, but the way *from* the tomb, the road that leads from the place of Jesus' victory into every corner of the world. And for this road we need a passport and a map, to open the way to new places and to assure us that our travelling is worth while.

The passport is the Easter story itself. Peter went into the tomb and saw the graveclothes; the other disciple went in, saw, *and believed*. Peter, of course, also believed soon afterwards; but, for the moment, let those two stand for people who've got their passports with them and people who haven't. When you arrive at the airport, whether to leave your own country or to land somewhere else, it's no good telling the customs officials that you do indeed possess a passport, but that it happens to be on the dressing table back home. You need it with you. All Peter could do was to stare dumbfounded. The other disciple saw and believed:

with that faith a new country was opened, a new possibility appeared before him, as it would for someone whose confiscated passport had at last been returned. Many in our society stand and stare at the Christian message, and don't know what to do with it. They remain imprisoned in the country of their own limited possibilities. But those who go in, and see, and believe, find, thrust into their hands, a passport which declares that all things are now possible. No country is barred to them; all roads are now open.

The passport allows you to start your journey. But the journey itself is often hard; the road is twisty and rough. We need a map to check that we really are going in the right direction. As such a map, I offer a little word of St Paul, right at the end of the chapter in which he discusses the meaning of Jesus' resurrection (1 Corinthians 15). At the end of his long argument, Paul does not conclude by saying 'so therefore we can be assured of life after death'. He says, rather, 'be steadfast, immovable, always abounding in the work of the Lord, since you know that, in the Lord, your labour is not in vain' (15.58).

The resurrection spreads out before us *the map of God's new world*. When Jesus of Nazareth came out of the tomb on Easter morning, in his transformed, renewed body, having gone through death itself and out the other side, he gave the world the first glimpse of the fact that God is in the business, not of abandoning this sad old world and taking us off to a disembodied heaven, but of redeeming, renewing, transforming this world, so that everything that has been good, lovely, just, holy, beautiful is enhanced, purified, ennobled, raised to new heights of glory. In that new world, as in Jesus' restored physical body, even the scars and wounds become signs of glory. Easter offers us a map of that new world, a map for explorers, a map to encourage us to get out there and get on with the task.

The point is this. What was *begun* with the resurrection of Jesus will be *continued* until it is thoroughly finished; every act of faith and love, of justice and mercy, of beauty and truth in this present world will be part of God's eventual new world. In the Lord, your labour is not in vain: what you do here in faith will stand, will last. Failure, cynicism, deconstruction and despair do not have the last word. They are the soldiers standing guard at the tomb, and when morning comes they are sound asleep. The passport of Jesus' bodily resurrection declares that you are free to travel; the map of God's new world declares that all your travelling in faith is worth while. With these as our guides, let us proceed on the way, or rather the ways, from the tomb.

Of the many possible ways from the tomb, I choose four to focus on briefly as our pilgrimage reaches its conclusion. The first is the way to Emmaus, where many pilgrims today pause for prayer, reflection and perhaps a celebration of the eucharist. Emmaus stands, in Luke's marvellous story, for the surprising personal meeting with Jesus.

Two disciples are going home, puzzled and downcast, on the evening of the first Easter Day. Their hopes have been shattered. Jesus himself joins them on the road; he explains to them what has happened; he comes home and breaks bread with them; they recognize him, and suddenly discover both passport and map for their new journeys. The first way from the empty tomb is the way to a surprising and healing meeting with the risen Jesus: a meeting to which every child, woman and man in the world is now invited.

This invitation has no conditions on it. Don't say 'Everything's gone wrong in my life, so it can't happen to me'; that is precisely where people are when Jesus meets them afresh. Don't say 'I don't understand any of it, so it can't happen to me'; Jesus comes precisely as the explainer. Don't say 'My life is complicated enough already without this religious stuff'; you might as well say 'I'm having a hard enough time finding the way as it is, without having to read a stupid map.' Don't say 'My life's too sad just now, so I can't bear any of that cheerful stuff'; the risen Jesus is recognized by the mark of the nails, and loves nothing better than to share and bear the sorrows of suffering people. This personal meeting with Jesus is for all.

The way to this personal meeting, this personal knowing, of Jesus, stands open before you today and every day. The empty tomb is your passport to it: Jesus is alive, he is risen, by his Spirit he is present, and he offers you a surprising and healing meeting with himself. And the empty tomb points to the map of God's future: this personal meeting with Jesus is not just a bit of navel-gazing spirituality, irrelevant to real life and ultimate destiny. In the Lord, your labour is not in vain. On the map of God's new world, the intimate, personal relationship with Jesus to which you are invited, of which the eucharist is both a sign and a means, is the beginning of a relationship to be finally consummated when, in his new world, we see and know him face to face. Just as lovers remember gladly the first stumbling beginnings of their courtship, so when we see Jesus face to face will we recall with delight our first meetings with him in the present. And in that new world the wounds of your own life will be, like the wounds of Jesus, the way we are recognized. Take your passport; take your map; and set out to meet your risen Lord. Don't put it off.

The second way from the tomb, as the disciples found, is the way back to the city. The city was the place of fear. They were hiding behind locked doors, afraid that the people who had come for Jesus would come for them too. And the city was the place of failure. It was where they had got it all wrong, where they had let Jesus down, where they had sworn blind that they didn't even know him. And now they were invited to go back to the locked upper room and to discover that Jesus came to meet them there, to bring them forgiveness for all that they had done, and new energy to open the locked doors, to go out in faith and hope and love.

Plenty of people suppose that Christian faith is a matter of covering up your fears, of pretending that you haven't really been a failure, of entering a world of make-believe, like children pulling the bedclothes over their heads, creating a cosy, warm little world from which reality is conveniently excluded. But that is the very opposite of the truth. Easter is about facing fears and discovering hope; Easter is about looking failure in the face and discovering forgiveness and new possibilities. With the empty tomb as your passport, you are encouraged and enabled to revisit your worst fears and failures, knowing that the Jesus who meets you there is the Jesus who will not scowl and make you feel worse than before, but who will embrace you and love you and give you a new start. And with the empty tomb as your map of the future, you can make that new start, knowing that in the Lord your labour is not in vain; that your new efforts to be loyal to him, to live for him, to love others with his love, however feeble they feel at the time, will remain and be enhanced in God's new world. And even the wounds and scars that you bear from past fear and failure will become, as Jesus' wounds have become, strange signs of hope and glory.

The third way from the tomb, as the Acts of the Apostles indicates, is the way to Judaea and Samaria, the countryside surrounding Jerusalem. In Jesus' day this was a place of great tension, between the Jews and the Samaritans, and between both of them and the occupying forces. Jesus' first followers did not go out into a comfortable world where people were sitting around looking for a new spirituality or theology, but into a world torn apart by hatred and suspicion, by the angry memory of atrocities, by land disputes, enemy occupation, and by a steep divide between rich and poor, possessors and dispossessed. And of course what some call 'Judaea and Samaria' today is the territory known officially to the United Nations and most of the world as the Occupied West Bank, where hatred and suspicion are still the order of the day, where atrocities and land disputes are daily occurrences, where possessors and dispossessed are still locked in resentful confrontation. And the way from the empty tomb is the way into precisely that country, taking the message of new life and new starts, the gospel of reconciliation and forgiveness.

This is not the place, and I am not the person, to suggest what that might mean in today's literal West Bank, today's Judaea and Samaria. (I shall offer my own reflections on that subject in the Epilogue.) But, as we all know, the sorry drama acted out there in the first century and in the twentieth is simply a microcosm of the drama that goes on all over God's world: in the Balkans, in Africa, in South-east Asia, in the former Soviet Union, in Latin America. And, of course, in our own 'enlightened' Western world, whether in northern Spain or Northern Ireland. We rejoice at the new steps forward that have been taken in various peace processes, and pray fervently that they may produce lasting success; but we are under no illusions as to the difficulties still faced, the seeming impossibility of convincing everybody that talk is better than terror, that kindness is better than killing, that forgiveness and new starts are real possibilities. Yet, as we have seen in South Africa, not least because of the steady and patient work of thousands of Christians there, forgiveness and reconciliation, though costly, are possible and are worth struggling for. Desmond Tutu, and thousands of other Christians, black, white and coloured, have taken their Easter passports seriously, and have declared that the door to reconciliation is not locked shut, that past bitterness and anger can be dealt with; and I dare to say that the work they have done and are doing is, in the Lord, not in vain, that they have sketched in part of the map of God's new world, to be enhanced and not done away with in the eventual new creation.

Most of us, of course, merely look on these enormous and earth-shaking political and social affairs from afar. But we face issues too, not so striking but none the less real and vital, in our local community life. Hatred and suspicion are habits of mind that spread like cancers through communities at every level, poisoning relationships, shutting down possibilities of healing and hope. Every city, every district, every parliamentary constituency, has the option of suspicion and confrontation, but also of forgiveness and reconciliation. If it can happen in South Africa, and even, please God, in Northern Ireland, it can happen anywhere. When we say 'Christ is risen, Alleluia!', we are seizing our passports to a new set of possibilities: to working creatively for peace and reconciliation, for justice and hope and new starts, in every community, every city hall, every council chamber, every parliamentary session. We are not just working for mutual tolerance; that is a low-grade eighteenth-century substitute for the real thing. Those who claim the empty tomb as their passport are working for the enrichment of a community life where mutual suspicion is replaced by deep respect and affirmation. Easter opens up new possibilities, and we who possess the passport are urged to explore them.

And those who are on the way from the empty tomb need also to remember the map. How easy to suppose that politics and community organization are just temporary patchwork solutions to keep chaos at bay! How easy to imagine, if you think of Christianity simply as a hope for life after death, to suppose that community work and organization doesn't have much lasting significance, since what matters is the eternal salvation of individual souls! But Paul's map gives the lie to that. 'Be steadfast, immovable, abounding in the work of the Lord, since you know that in the Lord *your labour is not in vain.*' Every act of justice and reconciliation; every time a politician votes with conscience rather than party; every step towards a truly caring society; every decision, individual or corporate, that has the stamp of God's love and peace upon it, is something that will be enhanced and ennobled in God's eventual new world. Nothing will be lost; all will resound to God's glory. The way to our own Judaea and Samaria, to reconciliation and hope in local communities and countries, stands open, and waits for individuals and politicians alike to take the passport and the map, and to go for it.

The fourth and final way from the empty tomb is the way across the sea, to the ends of the earth. In the Acts of the Apostles, it wasn't very long before those who believed in the resurrection of Jesus went with the good news far beyond their local communities. This was something the world needed to hear. The world, of course, was run by Caesar in Rome, and Caesar and his henchmen didn't take kindly to ambassadors from rival kings. But the apostles, as good Jews, believed that Israel's Messiah was the Lord of the whole world; and the resurrection had convinced them that Jesus was indeed Israel's Messiah. The fact that he had been crucified turned their Jewish expectation of a national kingdom inside out, meaning that this king would come into his kingdom, not by force of arms, but by suffering love. The way from the empty tomb, the new inside-out pilgrim way, led them out into the market-places and sea-ports, into the mountain ranges and council chambers, of the whole wide world, to declare that there is another king, another lord, another way of being human, a different God, a different set of possibilities, to those the sad and worried world had imagined.

Notice what has happened. The whole world has now become the Holy Land. Instead of defending or redefining a particular strip of sacred turf, Christianity declares in the name of the risen Jesus that the whole world is his domain, that at his name, one day, every knee shall bow. Those who find the way from the empty tomb discover that it, too, is the pilgrim way: that, having gone to the centre of the earth, to the city where God's love and the world's pain met together, they are then sent off as inside-out pilgrims, to discover God at work in the wider world, to recognize the face of Jesus in the faces of the poor, the prisoners, the dying, the debt-ridden, those without dignity and without hope, and as pilgrims *to worship Jesus there* by bringing his healing love wherever they go. With Calvary and Easter, the Holy Land has become the holy person, Jesus himself, who goes ahead of us into all the world, to the places of pain and despair, and summons us to follow him and work for reconciliation and hope.

Here too we need the passport and the map. We in the modern West are tempted every day to leave the passport on the dressing-table, to suppose that if anything good can be done in the world we somehow have to do it by ourselves, by our own little schemes and hatched-up plots. Not so. We go to the task with the Easter passport in our hands, the document which says that God has opened up new possibilities in the world, bringing light out of darkness and life out of death. And we are always tempted to imagine that cynicism and despair will triumph after all, that the tyrants and the rich, the oppressors and the bullies, will win in the end. Not so. Every step away from the tomb to announce Jesus' lordship to the wider world is marking out territory on the map of God's new world. In the Lord, your labour is not in vain. When God's new world is finally revealed, what you have done to bring healing and hope, beauty and joy to your bit of the world will shine out as a glorious part of the rich tapestry of the new creation. And the wounds and scars which result from announcing Jesus' lordship in a world where other lords guard their territory with tanks, bombs and laws will be the sign that we have fought Jesus' battles with Jesus' weapons.

One sort of pilgrimage ends, therefore, and a new sort of pilgrimage begins, with the empty tomb of Jesus. We are invited to walk the road now to a new personal relationship with Jesus himself; to the transformation of fear and failure into hope and fruitful labour; to the places in our own world where confrontation and suspicion wreck individual and social relationships; and into all the world with the news that the crucified Jesus is its rightful and healing Lord. We go on this pilgrimage in the sure knowledge that in God's new world all who have loved him here will be raised to new life, and all that has been done in his name will be enhanced and reaffirmed. Some of us have had, and will have, the chance to go on an actual pilgrimage, to see the sights for ourselves and allow them to challenge us to fresh prayer, thought and action. But all of us are summoned to go on this inside-out pilgrimage, following in the way of the Lord, day by day and year by year, until God's kingdom comes.

Epilogue: The Holy Land Today

ALL THAT I have said in this book would be just as relevant if the Holy Land, and Jerusalem in particular, were uninhabited save for the guardians of the shrines and the obligatory little boys selling postcards. Or, for that matter, if the entire land were at peace, inhabited by one people living in peace and justice amongst themselves and with their neighbours. But, notoriously, that is not the case, and it doesn't look like being the case for some while to come. What effect does this have on our pilgrimages, geographical and metaphorical?

We must avoid the natural reaction of Westerners who, perhaps forgetting Northern Ireland, are tempted to regard squabbles in the Balkans or the Levant as the result of silly backward peoples, or perhaps hot-tempered Mediterranean peoples, who can't learn to get along with one another, and whose running skirmishes (and worse) get in the way of our natural desire to experience the 'sabbath rest by Galilee, the calm of hills above'. How inconsiderate of them, we think, to throw bombs at each other when we simply want to come and pray! This, of course, is a typically modern and typically Western reaction. In the hopes of a more thought-out possibility, I want to reflect by way of conclusion on the reality of things on the ground in Israel and the West Bank today, and then to reflect on how this reality might affect pilgrimage to that land. And to everything that I shall now say I want to add: 'but it's actually far more complicated than that'.

Once upon a time there was a lady who rejoiced in a large family. Her husband was rich and well respected. His family used to live in a fine stately home in the country; impecunious ancestors had given it up several centuries ago, but the family still thought of it as theirs. One day, burglars broke into their current home. They shot the husband, raped and murdered the daughters, cut the throats of all the sons, and stole everything they possessed. The lady and one child miraculously escaped. Desperately seeking to make a new life, they discovered that the old family home seemed to be available. With help from a few friends, who felt guilty that no-one had heard the family's cries for help in their hour of need, they moved in, assuming that the few people living on the estate were servants. The lady married again, and in a short time had a new and flourishing family. However, to her dismay and alarm, some of the tenants on the estate seemed to resent her arrival, and were plotting to get rid of her. Why, she wondered, does the whole world seem to have it in for me? What have I done to deserve this? Why can't I just be left to live in peace after all I've suffered?

Now let's tell the story the other way round. Once upon a time there was a family who had lived in a great old house for so long that they'd almost forgotten they hadn't built it themselves. They loved the house and its grounds dearly; they knew every room, every nook and cranny, every stick and stone on the property. They had suffered much because of violent and abusive neighbours, and were reduced in circumstances to the point where some of the fine rooms in the house were shut up, and some fields left uncultivated. One day, to their alarm, a woman swept up the drive in a car, announced that she was in charge now, and proceeded to throw some of the family off the estate altogether, herding many of the rest into little encampments, while she took over the best parts of the house and grounds. When they protested, she called up her powerful friends, who gave her money to see her through. Now, a generation later, the family have grown used to her, but many, particularly the younger generation, are asking why they have to put up with this intolerable situation a moment longer.

No parable can begin to do justice to the complex reality. Centuries of European anti-Semitism came to their awful climax in the Holocaust (or, in Hebrew, the Shoah), when six million European Jews died. Some in the West knew and did nothing. Many knew little and cared less. Some cared but knew little. When the facts came to light, a huge head of steam built up, not least from horror, deep sympathy, and residual guilt either for conniving with anti-Semitism or at least for standing by and doing nothing. The Jews, millions felt, must have a homeland. Uganda was proposed. So was part of Argentina. But most Jews knew that only their ancient homeland, promised by God to Abraham, possessed by Joshua, would do. Many thousands had already emigrated there, often in defiance first of Turkish rule and then of the British mandate. In May 1948 the United Nations set up the new state of Israel.

Many of the early Jewish settlers genuinely believed the land was empty. 'A land without people for a people without a land' was their slogan. This, however, was far from the truth. The Palestinians were neither numerous nor strong, but they existed, real people living in real houses on real farms, running real businesses. They were ordered out, often with threats, sometimes with actual violence. In typical instances, they were given half an hour to get ready, and then bussed away, either over the border into Jordan (thereby creating huge new problems for that neighbour) or into specified towns such as Nazareth. They were not allowed

back. To this day there are Jews living in those Palestinians'
houses, tilling their fields, sleeping in their beds, eating off
their china, and quite likely quoting Deuteronomy to back
it all up: houses you did not build, fields you did not plant,
vineyards you did not grow. Two poignant pictures from
dozens stand out: a little boy persuading the bus-driver to
stop at his front gate so he could get his radio from the
house; an old man, told to pack up his belongings, going
instead out to his small garden to say a fond and sad
farewell to his two olive trees, which he and his forebears
had lovingly cultivated for countless generations.

The tale is too long to tell here, and far too complex,
intricate and many-sided. The Jews came in on the high
moral ground of their sufferings in the Holocaust: the Yad
Vashem memorial, in modern West Jerusalem, stands both
as a horrific reminder of the appalling sufferings of European
Jewry a generation ago and as a strong appeal for the moral
legitimacy of the present state of Israel. Every criticism of
Israel can at once be construed as a resurgence of anti-
Semitism. The Palestinians, with every passing year, claim
higher and higher moral ground, as many of them live in
dirty and squalid refugee camps, kept behind barbed wire
while sometimes, within their sight, new settlements, with
all modern conveniences, are built for Jewish immigrants to
live in (and to guard fiercely), and holiday resorts for them
to play in. The Jews lose moral ground every time another
settlement goes up in the West Bank, which the Orthodox
refer to as 'Judaea and Samaria', in defiance of United
Nations resolutions and of the spirit of the Oslo accord.
The Palestinians lose moral ground every time they
demonstrate in support of Saddam Hussein, every time
another Hamas suicide bomber blows himself up, taking
another dozen Israeli civilians with him. And we British

have little if any moral ground to stand on in the eyes of either Israel or Palestine. During the thirty-one years of the British mandate we managed to get ourselves in the bad books of both sides.

Among the Jews, of course, are a large minority, perhaps even a majority, who long for peace with their every breath, who would only too gladly give up some land for the sake of it, and who bitterly resent the importation from America of plane-loads of Orthodox cousins, fired up with passionate synagogue sermons from their ageing rabbis in Brooklyn, ready to arm themselves and take over the Promised Land. Jewish Israel is today a deeply divided nation. Among the Palestinians, of course, are a large minority, perhaps even a majority, who do not now want to see the Jews driven back into the sea; who would be happy to live and let live, to create a new situation in which all could live as neighbours. Policies shift, and people move with or against them: Yasser Arafat, once regarded as the classic Palestinian terrorist, is now the moderate, trying desperately to hold the centre in the fragmented little Palestinian homeland, while many to his left (or is it right?) see violence as the only solution. We in Britain are all too familiar with the spirals of violence and mistrust in Northern Ireland; multiply the recipe by about a hundred, add in a strong dose of Old Testament fanaticism on the one hand and Islamic fundamentalism on the other, stir vigorously in the cross-currents of global politics, and cook in a small overheated oven a hundred miles long and fifty miles wide. That is the beautiful and tragic country to which pilgrims still travel in search of the one true God.

I cannot here attempt to address the political situation further, though the partial parallels with Northern Ireland, and even with the former situation in South Africa are too close for comfort. What I sense a responsibility to do at the end of this book is to outline what all this means for the Christian pilgrim going to the Holy Land today.

There are thousands, perhaps millions of Christians in the world – I regularly meet them, read their writings, and get accosted by them after addressing meetings or services – who passionately believe that the return of the Jews to their ancient homeland, climaxing in 1948 and building on from there, is the God-given fulfilment of Old Testament prophecy. Many such people cherish particular schemes of what are referred to as the 'end times'. In such scenarios, texts from Ezekiel, Daniel and Revelation are brought together in schematic form and applied to twentieth-century political realities. They are regularly used to indicate that the long exile of the Jewish people, dating back to the destructions of Jerusalem first by the Babylonians and then by the Romans, will finally be undone, and that the new Jewish existence in Palestine, coming into public acceptance in 1948 and growing thereafter, will herald the dawn of the final day when Jesus Christ will return, will fight the great battle at Armageddon, and will set up his kingdom once and for all. The details vary with different interpretations, but the overall scheme is well known.

This scheme is, of course, well liked by Zionists. It engenders, from newspaper columns to plane-loads of tourists, unthinking support for the state of Israel and all that it is and does, so that any and every criticism of that state, even of its more obtuse and blatant right-wing actions, is met with the charge of anti-Semitism, of failing to understand the Bible properly, of failing to see God's hand in history. I was once at a conference at which, in the hearing of many Palestinian Arab Christians, an American Jewish Christian declared that the land belonged inalienably to her and her people. She graciously allowed that, according to

Deuteronomy, the Arabs could be permitted to stay – as long as they were made hewers of wood and drawers of water. Those who take such a position find themselves committed to great ambiguities. I once knew a young Jewish Christian in Montreal who believed passionately that the return of Jews to the Land was the fulfilment of biblical prophecy, heralding the return of Jesus. He applied to emigrate to Israel himself. In granting him permission, the authorities stipulated that he go through a ritual bath to renounce his Christianity. He and I talked about it and prayed about it together. He went ahead. Within a short time he was back, a sadder but not wiser man. The Promised Land was not like he had imagined it. Israeli Jews were not supposed to be Christians; if they were, they risked losing their citizenship. How could this be the fulfilment of prophecy?

Behind this muddled thinking lies, of course, a deep divide over how Christians should read the Old Testament. In what way, by what means, does this extraordinary book become our book? How can we claim that we, Jew and Gentile alike in the body of Christ, are the children of Abraham, the one people of promise? Is not this a denial of the specialness of Israel? Does it not constitute in itself the beginning of anti-Semitism? Such charges are regularly laid against Christians who claim such things, basing their claim on Paul, 1 Peter and other New Testament writings. But this is a case of being condemned if you do and condemned if you don't. Exactly the same charge is levelled against Christians who forget their Jewish roots, who construct a neo-Marcionite system in which Abraham and the covenant are left behind (Marcion was a second-century heretic who denied that the God revealed in Jesus was the same as the God of the Old Testament), who speak of Paul's doctrine of justification as Paul's attack on 'Judaism', who see 'the Jews' in themselves as the problem, and Christianity as the answer.

The New Testament itself, of course, from start to finish sees the gospel of Jesus as the fulfilment of all that God had promised to his people in the Old. On the road to Emmaus, Jesus expounded to the two puzzled disciples all the things in the scriptures which concerned himself. That remains the foundation of Christian existence.

One of the specific things on which the New Testament insists, again and again, is that in the life, death and supremely the resurrection of Jesus the promised new age has dawned. The return from exile has happened. 'All the promises of God', says Paul in 2 Corinthians 1.20, 'find their "yes" in him.' This is in fact the great Return, even though it doesn't look like people had thought it would. Instead of Israel as a political entity emerging from political exile, we are invited in the gospel to see Israel-in-person, the true king, emerging from the exile of death itself into God's new day. That is the underlying rationale for the mission to the Gentiles: God has finally done for Israel what he was going to do for Israel, so now it's time for the Gentiles to come in. That, too, is the underlying rationale for the abolition of the food laws and the holy status of the land of Israel: a new day has dawned in God's purposes, and the symbols of the previous day are put aside, *not* because they were a bad thing, now happily rejected, but because they were the appropriate preparatory stages in God's plan, and have now done their work. When I became a man, I put away childish things. Lift up your eyes, says Paul in Romans 8, and see how the promises to Abraham are to be fulfilled: not simply by a single race coming eventually to possess a single holy strip of turf, but by the liberation of the whole cosmos, with the beneficiaries, the inheritors of the promise, being a great number from every race and tribe and tongue, baptized and believing in Jesus Christ and indwelt by his Spirit.

To suggest, therefore, that as Christians we should support the state of Israel because it is the fulfilment of prophecy is, in a quite radical way, to cut off the branch on which we are sitting. It is directly analogous to the mistake of the Galatians, who thought that if they were members of Abraham's family they should go the whole way and get circumcised. It is similar to the mistake of which the Reformers accused the mediaeval Catholics, of supposing that in every Mass they were actually re-crucifying Jesus, when Jesus' death had been once and for all, never to be repeated, on Calvary. It is a way of saying that in the cross and resurrection God did not actually fulfil his whole saving purpose; that Jesus did not in fact achieve the fulfilment of Old Testament prophecy; that his resurrection was not the start of God's new age; that Acts is wrong, Romans is wrong, Galatians is wrong, the letter to the Hebrews is wrong, Revelation is wrong. Say that if you like, but don't claim to be Christian in doing so.

In particular, as pilgrims we must take with the utmost seriousness the fact that almost all Christians living in the Holy Land today are Palestinians. Yes, there are some Jewish Christians, some brave souls living their faith openly, and, I have it on good authority, many others who practise their allegiance to Jesus as Messiah behind locked doors, as certain of their forebears did between the first Easter and the first Pentecost. But most of those who worship God in Christ day by day and week by week in the Holy Land today are Palestinian Arabs: people like Elias Chacour, Naim Ateek and Audeh Rantisi, all Anglican priests (which is why I happen to know them), who have had the courage to speak up and speak out for justice and freedom, for justice for Jews and Arabs alike, to speak out against torture, against the building of new settlements, against the systematic brutalization of a whole people which then provokes more of the violence it condemns.

What does it do to Christians like that when they see massive American funding pouring in to the state of Israel, sustaining the regime that is oppressing them? What does it do to them when they hear again and again that many Christians are backing the state that is doing its best to eliminate them? Many Palestinian Christians are now in exile, in America or elsewhere, and do not expect to return. They have given up the struggle. Many are tempted to make common cause with their Muslim neighbours, the Cross and the Crescent united against the Star of David. Yet many know that even if the Arab world got together and succeeded where they failed in the wars of 1949, 1967 and 1974 – in other words, if they managed to eliminate or marginalize the state of Israel altogether – then the battle would be on to establish in its place an Islamic republic of Palestine similar to that in Iran and elsewhere, in which, as in many Muslim countries, Christianity would be at far greater risk than it is from the present Israeli government. They feel themselves to be between the devil and the deep blue sea. They are our brothers and sisters: the 'living stones', as they call themselves, ignored by many tourists, especially those who go on one of the Israeli-government-sponsored tourist packages, but very much alive, very much present, maintaining their dignity, their worship, and their hope, though with increasing difficulty. 'Is it nothing to you,' they say, 'all you who pass by?' If we go to worship in the Holy Land, we dare not ignore our brothers and sisters in pain all around us.

When we go on pilgrimage today, then, we do not go in order to comment on or criticize other people for their inability to solve political problems. God knows we can't solve our own, which are much smaller and less rooted in history. Of course, we will grieve over injustice, oppression and violence wherever it occurs and whoever instigates it; but in highly complex situations it behoves us to go with our eyes and ears open, ready to learn rather than to condemn. But as pilgrims we go, above all, to pray. In the same passage where Paul speaks of God's intention to make the whole world his Holy Land, to renew and liberate the whole of creation, he also speaks of the whole creation at present groaning in travail; and then he declares that we who have the first fruits of the Spirit groan inwardly as we, too, wait for our final redemption (Romans 8.18–27). It is in that context that he says that all things work together for good to those who love God (8.28). What can he mean?

He means, I think, that our vocation as Christians includes the vocation *to be in prayer at the place where the world is in pain*. We are not to expect to pray only at places of great beauty, stillness and peace. We are not to look only for selfish refreshment, to top up our own spiritual batteries while forgetting everyone else. We are to stand or kneel at the place where the world, and particularly our brother and sister Christians, are in pain and need, and, understanding and feeling their sufferings, to pray with and for them, not knowing (as Paul again says) what precisely to ask for, but allowing the Spirit to pray within us with groanings that cannot come into articulate speech. We are called, in other words, to become in ourselves places where the living, loving and grieving God can be present at the places of pain in his world and among his children. We are called to discover the other side of pilgrimage: not only to go somewhere else to find God in a new way, but to go somewhere else in order *to bring God in a new way to that place*, not by tub-thumping evangelism or patronizing, well-meaning but shallow advice, but by our presence, our grief, our sympathy, our encouragement, our prayer.

As we do this, in going to the Holy Land today, we find the three things I said about pilgrimage in the introduction to this book reinforced and given particular direction.

Pilgrimage is a teaching aid: at this level, it teaches us not only about the roots of our faith, but about the ways in which injustice still rampages through communities, some of them within our own family. It opens our eyes to see God's world the way it is, rather than the way we would like to imagine it. Second, pilgrimage is a way of prayer: both a way of drinking in the presence and love of God in Christ, as we visit places particularly associated with him, and also now a way of standing at the place of pain, at the foot of the cross literally and metaphorically, holding on to that pain in the presence of God in Christ, not knowing what the solution will be but only that God is there, grieving with and in us, in a perpetual Holy Week at the heart of the Holy Land. Third, pilgrimage is a way of discipleship: both to be reinforced in our own daily life and work as Christians, and now also to be reinforced in thinking, working, speaking, writing and praying for justice and peace to be restored to the Middle East, to Northern Ireland, to the Sudan, to God's entire creation.

We do not go on pilgrimage, then, because we have the answers and want to impose them. That would make us crusaders, not pilgrims; the world has had enough of that, and I dare say God has had enough of that. We go on the pilgrim way, we follow the way of the Lord, because he himself is the way – and, as he said himself, the truth and the life as well. We go to meet him afresh, to share his agony, and to pray and work for the victory he won on the cross to be implemented, and for his way to be followed, in Israel and Palestine, in our own countries, and in the whole world.

Quotation Sources

Quotations from the Bible are the author's own translation.

pp. 19–20, 'Last night, going to bed alone': Edwin Muir, *An Autobiography*, Hogarth Press, 1954, p. 246.

pp. 21–2, 'Saint Paul is often criticised': John Betjeman, 'The Conversion of St Paul', in *Uncollected Poems*, John Murray, 1982, pp. 67–70.

p. 36, 'In order to arrive'; p. 37, 'I said to my soul': T. S. Eliot, *Four Quartets*, in *The Complete Poems and Plays*, Faber & Faber, 1969, pp. 181, 180.

p. 47, 'O Sabbath rest by Galilee': John Whittier, 'Dear Lord and Father of Mankind', *The New English Hymnal*, no. 353.

p. 55, 'Pride of man and earthly glory': Robert Bridges, 'All my hope on God is founded', *The New English Hymnal*, no. 333.

p. 71, 'O World invisible'; p. 74, 'The drift of pinions' and 'The angels keep their ancient places'; p. 77, 'But (when so sad thou canst not sadder)'; Francis Thompson, 'The Kingdom of God', in *Selected Poems of Francis Thompson*, Jonathan Cape, 1929, pp. 131f.

p. 73, 'Father Seraphim gripped me': Nicholas Motovilov

(1809–32) in Valentine Zander, *St Seraphim of Sarov*, trans. Sr Gabriel Anne, SPCK, 1975, pp. 90–2.

p. 97, 'Great God, in Christ you call our name'; p. 106, 'Then take the towel': Brian Wren, *Piece Together Praise: A Theological Journey*, © 1975, 1995 Stainer & Bell Ltd.

pp. 99–100, 'This morning I have had my annual': John Carden, *Empty Shoes: A Way in to Pakistan*, Highway Press, 1971, pp. 34–6.

p. 101, 'This is my friend': Samuel Crossman (1624–83), 'My song is love unknown', *The New English Hymnal*, no. 86.

p. 103, 'The wounded surgeon'; p. 104, 'The dripping blood': T. S. Eliot, *Four Quartets*, in *The Complete Poems and Plays*, Faber & Faber, 1969, p. 181f.